Bismillah and Bean Pie

Bismillah & Bean Pies

Bismillah and Bean Pies

And Say: My Lord Increase Me in Knowledge- Quran
20:114

Bismillah and Bean Pies

© Asad El Malik

All Rights Reserved. No part of this publication may be reproduced, stored in a retrieval system, or transmitted in any form or by any means, electronic, mechanical, photocopying, recording, or otherwise without the prior permission of the Copyright owner.

Published in 2016
Muslim Fresh Publishing
New Orleans, LA
www.asadelmalik.com

ISBN-13:978-1537088983
ISBN-10:153708898X

Bismillah and Bean Pies

This page left blank intentionally

Bismillah and Bean Pies

Forward   7

Author's Preface   15

Islam, West Africa,
& American Slavery   29

Marcus, Muslims,
and Missionaries   56

Particularism, Moorish Science, and
the Nation of Islam   95

Bismillah and Bean Pies

Forward

Bismillah and Bean Pies

There is a Hadith quoted by Abū Hurayrah that says the Prophet (peace be upon him) spoke the following words: "Islam began strange, and it will become strange again just like it was at the beginning, so blessed are the strangers." [Sahīh Muslim] I have read several of the commentaries written by Islamic scholars concerning this Hadith. None of those I read have made a connection between this Hadith and the descendants of the Africans who were taken from their homeland by Europeans either by force or after being sold by some other Africans. As a student of the Teachings of the Most Honorable Elijah Muhammad I believe that we are the people that fulfill the prophecy written in the Book of Genesis chapter 15 verses 12-16 which says:

As the sun was going down, Abram fell into a deep sleep, and a terrifying darkness came down over him. 13 Then the Lord said to Abram, "You can be sure that your descendants will be strangers in a foreign land, where they will be oppressed as slaves for 400 years. 14 But I will punish the nation that enslaves them, and in the end they will come away with great wealth. 15 (As for you, you will die in peace and be buried at a ripe old age.) 16 After four generations your descendants will return here to this land, for the sins of the Amorites do not yet warrant their destruction."

One of the definitions of the word strange is, "different from what is usual, normal, or expected." The various practices or expressions of Islam by Blacks in America looks strange to our brothers and sisters from the East. Many of them look from afar and see Blacks in America similarly to the way a big brother sees his litter brother trying to grow into his own. They look on with the thought that we need to come to them to learn how to properly practice or live "The Deen." The Honorable Minister Louis Farrakhan stated that once during his travels in the Middle East a Muslim who is held in high regard told him, "I am happy to see that you all have begun to practice our religion." The Honorable Minister Louis Farrakhan pointed out to him Allah's words in the Holy Quran which says that Islam is the nature of man (Surah 30:30) and with that being so Islam is the very NATURE of the Original man and woman of whom the Black man and woman in America are direct descendants. I remember in college reading a book written about Islam and the African American experience, where an Imam from the Middle East who leads a mosque that has a significant number of Muslims of African descent marveled at how many of the most faithful adherents to the principles of Islam in the masjid were the Blacks that had accepted the faith. It is easy to us because Islam is our natural way of life. The name of our natural way of life was revealed to Prophet Muhammad (PBBUH) 1,400 years ago.

For many of our own people here in America, the religion of Islam looks strange as well. You can hear it in their questions or comments when they meet Muslims, "Why do Muslims bend down on the floor to pray? Why do Muslim women have to be covered? Who is Allah? Why haven't I read that in the Bible? Muhammad ain't like Jesus! What made you want to practice that Islam /Muslim stuff?" Their disconnect from our history and original way of life makes what they see, our very nature, as strange. Over the years I have watched people who do not consider themselves to be Muslims be moved by the beautiful sound of the Adhan and al-Fatiha being recited. Many speak about how hearing it touched their very core. It does that because Islam is their very core, they just do not realize it because they have been separated from their natural way, which now looks strange, but as Prophet Muhammad (PBUH) says, "blessed are the strangers."

    This is one of the benefits of this book written by my brother, Asad El Malik. It will introduce the reader to the long history of Islam in the lives of Black people here in America and in Africa. His book also highlights the role Islam has played in influencing Black Nationalism in America. Brother Asad does his very best to discuss the presence and influence of all individuals, groups and organizations who used their understanding of Islam to improve the wretched condition in which white supremacy placed them. Some may take issue with some of those who are mentioned in this book and question if what they taught was Islam at all. To those who can't see the Hand of Allah at work, I would only ask them to envision what the condition of Black people in America would be if these individuals, groups, and organizations never existed. I rather not discuss such hypothetical situations, because in the end, I see all of those who strive to live our original way of life as being a part of the fulfillment of the Hadith that speaks about the Sun of Islam rising in the West. Some Islamic scholars believe that this means the Earth would cease to rotate in its current direction, and begin spinning in the alternate direction in order to make the physical Sun rise in the West. I respectfully disagree. Instead, I see it referencing the rise of Islam from a place that has worked to put out the Light of Islam since its early encounter with it – The West. This book is necessary, because we who practice Islam, regardless of the school of thought, must not allow all of the literature that is written about its beginning, growth and spread in America to be told solely by those who do not practice the faith. As the Prophet was compelled to pick up the sword to fight against the enemies of the budding community in Medina, we need to begin to start picking up our pens to combat the propaganda which is part of the war against Islam. Our fight should not just remain in the field of academia. As Muslims, we need to demonstrate the majesty of Islam in our business dealings, our marriages, family lives and in the transformations of the communities where our Houses of Worship are located. The more we do this, the more we knock out the brains of falsehood and give the world a true example of the deen. The more our people and others will begin to realize that Islam is that Old Time Religion, that is sung about in the numerous churches throughout the world.

Brother Willie Muhammad
Student Minister of Muhammad
Mosque No. 46
New Orleans, La.

Bismillah and Bean Pies

Preface

Bismillah and Bean Pies

Bean pies have become synonymous with African American Islamic communities. The custard pie was introduced to the black palate by the Nation of Islam, an Islamic organization with black nationalist teachings, as an alternative to the sweet potato pie. The sweet potato was not in accord with the dietary recommendations of Elijah Muhammad's book "How to Eat to Live". The bean pie has become as much emblematic of Muhammad's organization as the bow tie. Although its genesis is in the Nation of Islam, the bean pie has grown to be a part of every African American Islamic expression. It, more than any other item, symbolizes the unique Muslim culture developed by blacks in America. The bean pie in many ways mirrors Islam in black America. Both find their roots in black nationalism and are a deviation from the overarching black culture in the United States.

Islam in black America evolves as a response to shifting societal conditions taking place within

Bismillah and Bean Pies

African American communities in the nineteenth and twentieth centuries. More than any other religion, Islam was used by African Americans as a means of gaining a cultural, historical, and national identity. The embrace of Islamic teachings often came with a rejection of the status quo in American society. The expression of Islam developed by African Americans was essentially a black protest religion in opposition to racism and white supremacy. A conversion to Islam often became associated with a moral, theological, philosophical, and political exeunt from the American societal stage. The black expression of Islam is at once an attempt to redefine black religious life and a social movement towards liberation. "African American Islam emerges as a religious practice in an urban, northern landscape that, at once, announces a different set of pieties and a new religious and political identity. As such, Islam among African Americans has always been a sign, a symbolic language bound up with a deep-seated suspicion of

Christian practice and a healthy skepticism about the U.S. nation-state, both of which are implicated in the evils of white supremacy." [1]

Theologian James H. Cone formularized Black Liberation Theology within the Christian context to address the unique experience and relationship that African Americans have with the church and he crafted a theology that directly confronted racism and white supremacy. Cone's Black Liberation Theology was directly influenced and was enacted as a response to the black Islamic liberating narrative that was being propagated by the Nation of Islam in particular. Just as Cone recognized a need to have a Christian expression that was responsive to African American concerns, black Muslims decades before Cone, articulated and expiated an Islamic expression that addressed the unique experience of African American Muslims. From the very

---

[1] Glaude Jr., Eddie S. African American Religion: A Very Short Introduction. Oxford: Oxford University Press, 2014.

beginning of the emergence of Islam in Black America, the experience of black people dictated how they expressed Islam. The idiosyncratic experience of African Americans within in the context of American white supremacy demanded an Islamic expression that addressed and engaged their condition. This unique expression, or particularism, is discussed in depth in chapter three.

Islam's history in the Americas dates back to at least the 1500s with some suggestion of an even earlier arrival. It is believed by some that the Muslim Abu Bakr II of Mali abdicated his throne and set sail to North America. There is no documentation to collaborate this story but it has persisted in African American Islamic folklore. "By the late 1500s, common Muslim-sounding names such as Hassan, Osman, Amar, Ali, and Ramadan appeared in Spanish language colonial documents. In the seventeenth and eighteenth centuries, as Job Ben Solomon's

Bismillah and Bean Pies

biography proves, the question is definitively settled. Various documents by and about American Muslims were published in English and other languages. This evidence establishes that Muslims from all Islamic regions of West Africa were present throughout the Americas during the colonial period." [2]

One of the most fascinating and interesting stories is that of Abd-Al-Rahman Ibrahima. He was a West African Muslim, of noble ancestry, and a military leader from what is now Guinea. Abd-al-Rahman was well learned and versed in Quranic surahs and could speak several languages including Arabic. He was most likely educated in Timbuktu and Jenne, which were centers of Islamic teachings in West Africa. His story, which will be explored in chapter one, is a fascinating tale of intelligence and endurance. He spent years as a slave but was eventually freed. He would spend the next months of his life on the lecture

---

[2] Curtis, EE Muslims In America: A Short History. Oxford: Oxford University Press, 2009

circuit in an attempt to raise money to free his children. He eventually returned to Africa but soon died. His notoriety as the "Moroccan Prince" may have popularized an idea that black Americans were descendants of Moors, a manifestation of this idea will be explored in this book in chapter three as the author examines the Moorish Science Temple.

    For enslaved African Muslims, isolation afforded them more opportunity to keep their Islamic faith and practices intact if they were able to be in communities with other practicing Muslims. For example, in communities like St. Simons Island and Sapelo Island, African traditions were able to be maintained including Islam. By the early 1900s, immigrants from other the parts of the Muslim world arrived in the United States. One of the most prominent and well known was the Indian musician and religious leader, Inayat Khan. He was a Sufi Muslim that traveled the country to entertain. Khan, like most of his contemporary Muslim immigrants, made little effort to engage or proselytize African Americans. An exception to this practice was Mufti Muhammad Sadiq who arrived as a missionary with the sole purpose to spread Islam in America. He was a follower of the teachings of Ahmad and the Ahmadiyya Islamic sect. The significance of this will be explored in chapter two. Sadiq believed and promoted the idea of equality and cultural agency for all men including African Americans. This idea was virtually unheard of in the white Christians teachings to which most blacks had been exposed. The Ahmadiyya newspaper, the Moslem Sunrise often pointed out the need for black Americans to withdraw from Christianity and to embrace Islam. Christianity, at the time, was associated with the Ku Klux Klan, Southern Democrats, and in many ways stood in opposition to the desires of Arican Americans. The racial climate made easy the task of convincing African Americans that the white Church was not in the best interest of black people. The Moslem

Sunrise editorialized "You need a religion which teaches manliness, self-reliance, self-respect, and self-effort." This is an early example of particularism in the black Islamic expression and presents the faith not only as a religious system but as a means of establishing masculinity, identity, agency and independence all of which became inseparable principles in the ideology of Black Nationalism and consequently Islam in Black America.

    Two African American men from the Caribbean can, arguably, be credited with Islam and Black Nationalism taking their "courtship" to the next level. Marcus Garvey was the founder and leader of the Universal Negro Improvement Association which stated aim was to unify Africans in the Diaspora and create an independent state in Africa. Garvey is considered the father of Black Nationalism and he held influence in many black communities in America and the Caribbean. He was mentored by Duse Muhammad Ali, a Muslim newspaper editor. The result of this relationship can be seen in much of Garvey's teachings, subtly if not overtly. Many Ahmadi leaders also courted Garvey to embrace Islam as the official religion of the movement. Prior to Garvey, another Caribbean man, Wilmot Blyden, also promoted the idea of Islam as the religion of black liberation and viewed the faith through the prism of Pan-Africanism.

By the 1920s, African Americans began to establish their own Islamic ideas independent of the Ahmadiyya or Sunni tradition. Timothy Drew otherwise known as Noble Drew Ali was an African American Islamic leader, possibly the first to establish a unique African American Islamic identity. Ali's Moorish Science Temple was established in Chicago in 1919. "But from the beginning, the label of Islam worked more like a sign of difference from white Christianity than a description of actual religious practices. What distinguished members of the group was not their practice of the five pillars of Islam, but their distinctive embrace of a national identity and creed that called into question their allegiance to the U.S. nation-state. Ali claimed that African Americans were not "Negroes" but "Asiatics," descendants of Moroccans who "could trace their genealogy to Jesus, a descendant of "the ancient Canaanites, the Moabites, and the inhabitants of Africa."[3] Ali taught that Islam was the original religion of African Americans and he sought to separate from whites. He taught his followers to practice a strict moral code and expounded ideas of Black Nationalism claiming that black Americans nationality was Moorish. He elevated himself to the level of a prophet and grew a large following in the midwestern United States. The Moorish Science Temple can be considered the proto-Islamic expression born out of the black American experience.

There can be no serious discussion of Islam in America

---

[3] Curtis, EE Muslims In America: A Short History. Oxford: Oxford University Press, 2009

Bismillah and Bean Pies

without the mentioning of Wallace D. Fard (Fard Muhammad), Elijah Poole (Elijah Muhammad), and the Nation of Islam. These two men and the organization they built loom large when discussing Islam in the West particularly through the prism of Black Nationalism. In 1930 Wallace D. Fard, possibly influenced by Garvey, the Ahmadi, and Drew Ali, started teaching a new expression of Islamic particularism in the black communities in Detroit. Much like the Ahmadi before him, he tailored his message to be more attractive to the newly arriving black migrant workers. The organization's name 'Nation of Islam', was a literal merger of black nationality with Islam. Whereas Drew Ali claimed a Moorish nationality, Fard made Islam the nationality of his followers. Fard's chief student was Elijah Muhammad who ran the organization from 1934-1975. Muhammad taught that black people were the first people on Earth and that an evil scientist named Yakub created the white race through genetic engineering. According to Muhammad, this white race was created to be the opposite of the original black people of planet Earth and eventually enslaved the black people and, according to Muhammad, converted them into Christians. Elijah Muhammad, more than any single person, married Black Nationalism with Islam and taught a complete formulation of an Islamic protest religion. Members of the Nation of Islam were taught not only religion but economics, business, politics, military training, sewing, strict dietary codes and Muhammad, like Garvey and Blyden before him, taught the need for independence. The teachings of Elijah Muhammad became known as "nation building." Whereas Marcus Garvey sought to establish a nation in Africa, Muhammad sought to establish a "nation within a nation". The Nation of Islam was attractive to African Americans on many levels. It offered political, social, and religious commonality much like any other nation.

From the very first African Muslims to arrive in North America

Bismillah and Bean Pies

to the rise of the Nation of Islam, Islam has been propagated and viewed through the prism of Black Nationalism. Islam became viewed more than just a religion but a social, political, and nationalist movement. Islamic symbols became intertwined with ideas of self-sufficiency, political and economic independence.

Bismillah and Bean Pies

Chapter One: Islam, West Africa, and American Slavery

Bismillah and Bean Pies

The discussion of Islam in the United States starts in West Africa in the Islamic nations along the shores and parts of the interior. It was from this region that Africans were captured and sold into slavery in the Americas. The region of the world is rich in Islamic traditions including Islamic dynasties, famous emperors, and highly advanced Islamic centers of learning. Much like the Islamic expression that emerged from the enslaved descendants of West Africans in the Americas, Islam in the region is a unique formulation complete with saints, rituals, and folklore only found in West African Islam. For example, in Senegal Amadou Bamba is venerated as a saint in the Sufi orders. Bamba was a Sufi religious leader that lead a struggle against French colonization. He also produced a prolific amount of poems and teachings on the Quran. After his death in 1927, many of the followers of his Mouride brotherhood elevated him to sainthood. He is often referred to as the "servant of the messenger" and is considered a "reviver of the faith". Millions of

Bismillah and Bean Pies

Senegalese Muslims travel annually to Touba, the city founded by Bamba, and worship. Bamba's poetry is recited daily by millions of Muslims. This expression of Islam is another example of particularism, a phenomenon of groups creating specific and unique practices, rituals, and beliefs centered on core Islamic principles. The experience of Sufi Senegalese Muslims dictated their expression.

Islam arrived in West Africa as early as the eighth century. In the eleventh century Senegal, under the rule of War Diaby, and Mali, under the rule of Kosoy became the first two West African Muslim countries. Soon, Islam spread to every part of the region with significant populations in every area and Muslim majorities in the present day countries of Mali, Senegal, Nigeria, Niger, and Cote d'Ivoire. There are several theories on why Islam spread through West Africa. "Some emphasize economic motivations, others highlight the draw of Islam's spiritual message, and a number stress the prestige and influence of Arabic literacy in facilitating state building."[4] Berbers from North Africa also played a key role in the introduction of Islam to West Africa through trade routes that were established below the Sahara. The main area of convergence between North Africa and West Africa was the Sahel. What is clear is that Islam was not spread by the sword, which is the prevailing mythology promoted by some Afro-centrists. Cheikh Anta Diop refutes these claims in his work Precolonial Black Africa. Diop wrote that Islam was "promulgated peacefully, at first by solitary Afro-Berber travelers to certain black kings and notables, who then spread it about...What is to be emphasized here is the peaceful nature of this conversion, regardless of the legend surrounding it."[5]

---

[4] Hill, Margari The Spread of Islam in West Africa: Containment, Mixing, and Reform from the Eighth to the Twentieth Century. Stanford: Stanford University, 2009

[5] Diop, Cheik A. Precolonial Black Africa. Illinois: Chicago Review Press, 1987

Bismillah and Bean Pies

A practice of containment was the initial response to Islam by West Africans. Muslims were isolated to small communities. For example, Muslims were allowed to trade in Ghana but were not allowed to stay overnight in the city. This allowed Ghana to benefit from the Muslim traders but prevented the Muslims from establishing agency and permanency.

While Islam became a powerful influence in West Africa, it was also influenced by the cultural customs and traditions of the populace. Spirituality and mysticism played an important role in many West African religious traditions and the introduction of Sufism to West Africa may have coincided with these beliefs. Cultural experiences were incorporated into Islamic practice. For example, in Malian Islamic communities ancestor veneration, a practice of some pre-Islamic African religions, became a common practice. Some West African Muslims would make salaat but saw no conflict with an animal sacrifice to ward off evil

Bismillah and Bean Pies

spirits. This flexibility, adaptability, and familiarity of practice made a conversion to Islam easy in many cases. As in many pre-Islamic African religious traditions, "circumcision, polygamy, communal prayers, divination, and amulet making also were present in Islam."[6] This mixing phase created a new and distinctly West African expression of Islam. In fact, Sonni Ali, the Muslim ruler of Songhay, "Persecuted Muslim scholars who criticized pagan practices."[7] Later, more dogmatic Muslims like the Almoravids attempted to impose more traditional Islamic practices and rid the integration of West African cultural practices.

The conversion of many West Africans to Islam also connected the region to the greater Islamic world and increased trade and

---

[6] Diouf, Sylviane A. *Servants of Allah: African Muslims Enslaved in the Americas*. New York: New York UP, 1998

[7] Hill, Margari The Spread of Islam in West Africa: Containment, Mixing, and Reform from the Eighth to the Twentieth Century. Stanford: Stanford University, 2009

communication with the Arab lands to the East. The ability to speak Arabic and make salaat was perceived as beneficial to West African traders and merchants who were trading salt and gold to Muslims. "Islam facilitated long-distance trade by offering useful sets of tools for merchants including contract law, credit, and information networks."[8]

Furthermore, the Islamic tradition of reading and reciting the Quran and using the Quran as the source of educational study increased literacy. Many West African Muslims could read and write Arabic as well as their local languages. Non-Muslims also benefitted from the madrasa in their communities by sending their children there to learn Arabic. The introduction of Islam into West Africa drastically increased literacy and brought an increased level of

---

[8] Hill, Margari The Spread of Islam in West Africa: Containment, Mixing, and Reform from the Eighth to the Twentieth Century. Stanford: Stanford University, 2009

erudition to the population. Arabic became the language of scholarship and many manuscripts were written using Arabic. Muslims "had the crucial skill of written script, which helped in the administration of kingdoms." This literacy amongst the West African Muslim would later come to their benefit during their sojourn in America.

Under Muslim leadership, empires in West Africa were established and expanded exponentially. There is no greater illustration of a West African imperial state than the empire of Mali. Mali was founded by Sundiata in the 1200s but it was under the rule of Mansa Musa that the empire became famous for its wealth of gold and Islamic scholarship. Musa was a fourteenth-century emperor that amassed the largest fortune ever known to man, a stunning $400 billion dollars (adjusting for inflation). His wealth was the result of Mali's vast natural resources. Mali, at the time, was home to one of the world's largest gold and salt deposits.

Bismillah and Bean Pies

Under Musa, the empire expanded its borders from the Atlantic Ocean to the Niger River. The empire encompassed a land mass of a half million square miles. Musa's predecessor, Mansa Abu Bakar II, is said to have abdicated his throne to explore the end of the Atlantic Ocean. Egyptian scholar Al-Umari wrote of the abdication and subsequent exploration of Mansa Bakar II which lead to Musa's ascent to the throne.

Musa reigned over a prosperous and powerful empire. He ordered the erection of extravagant palaces and masjids. Yet his most impressive feat was what he did outside of his country. His epic pilgrimage to Mecca is one of the most fascinating tales known to man. The sheer size of his caravan and the amount of items that were transported from the Mali to the Arabian City of Mecca is mind boggling. According to David W. Tschanz's Lion of Mali: The Hajj of Mansa Musa:

Bismillah and Bean Pies

"Leading the host were 500 heralds, clad in Persian silk and bearing four foot-long golden staff glistening in the sun and nearly blinding anyone who looked at them. Next came the royal guards some bearing spears and swords, others the flags of their empire...trudging solemnly behind him(Musa) were 80 camels, each bearing 300 pounds (140 kg) of gold – the modern equivalent of $576,000,000 – extracted from the mines of West Africa. There were 60,000 porters, and a retinue of 12,000 of the king's personal slaves. The king's senior wife herself brought 500 maids. In a move to discourage any ideas of insurrection, Mansa Musa ordered the leading citizens and officials of each province to journey with him and they brought their slaves and retainers."[9]

Mansa Musa's 3000-mile journey was not only impressive

---

[9] Tschanz, David W. Lion of Mali: The Hajj of Mansa Musa. http://www.academia.edu/1593503/
Lion_Of_Mali_The_Hajj_of_Mansa_Musa 2012

because of the size of his caravan but also that he built masjids along the way and gave away large sums of gold to the people he encountered. It is said that Musa gave away so much gold in Cairo and Mecca that the price of gold tanked due to vast supply. "It would take 20 years for the price of gold to recover."[10]

The narrative of Musa is often dominated by the tale of his hajj, but his domestic policies as a ruler were equally remarkable. His reign was marked by massive expansion. At its largest, the empire encompassed modern day Mali, Senegal, parts of Mauritania and Guinea. Musu made Islam the official religion and used it as the way of unifying the different ethnic groups in Mali. He established schools throughout the empire, built libraries, imported and employed Islamic scholars from around the Muslim world. This investment of money and intellectual capital made

---

[10] Tschanz, David W. Lion of Mali: The Hajj of Mansa Musa. http://www.academia.edu/1593503/Lion_Of_Mali_The_Hajj_of_Mansa_Musa 2012

the University of Timbuktu(Sankore) an Islamic 'Ivy League' institution. Muslim theologians and jurists from all over the Islamic world went to the University of Timbuktu to produce all levels of scholarship. Later, Songhay became the largest West African empire ever. The empire was marked by Islamic expansion. The Great Mosque of Jenne was erected during this period and remains the world's largest earthen building.

Slavery

The institution of slavery is probably as old as human existence. The ancient civilizations of Egypt, Babylon, Greece, and Rome all had slavery in some form. During the Middle Ages, Christian Europeans enslaved other Europeans including the Slavs. The word "Slavs" may come the Latin "sclavus"meaning slave which indicates the level of enslavement the Slavic people endured. Other Europeans such as the Irish, Welsh, Russians, and

Greeks were also enslaved in large numbers in medieval Europe. Slavery also existed in West Africa long before the Transatlantic Slave Trade. Throughout the region slavery was multifarious. Many of the pre-Islamic African religions did not prohibit slavery and some ethnic groups would enslave others mostly during wartime. Islamic law added another dimension to slavery in the region. West African slavery was never based on skin color or race rather religion and ethnicity were often used as justification for enslavement. For Muslims, the question of who could be enslaved became a debated topic. One of the most noted Islamic minds was Ahmad Baba. Baba was an Islamic jurist and writer. His fatwas (legal opinions) on slavery were some of the most important in Islamic history. In his work entitled "The Ladder of ascent towards the law concerning imported blacks" Baba argued that Islamic law dictates that fidelity (acceptance of Islam) was the determining factor for enslavement. Baba stated, "let it be known that infidelity, whether on the part of Christians, Jews, idolaters, Berbers, Arabs, or any other individual notoriously rebellious to Islam, is the only justification for slavery; there is no distinction to be made between miscreants, Sudanese or not."[11]

There was no uniform slavery in West African Islamic societies. The institution was implemented in various ways throughout the area but there were some common factors. Enslavement was mainly a result of a war, crime, or debt. Also, the employment of slaves was not limited to labor. Slaves in West Africa were also advisors, soldiers, tax collectors, and other professionals. By most accounts, slaves were treated well and manumission happened often. Islamic law limited the reasons one could be enslaved and protected Muslims from enslavement by other Muslims. "The West African Muslims largely followed the rule that prohibited them from selling their brethren, as was unanimously

---

[11] Moreau, Rene L. Africains Musulmans. Paris: Presence Africaine, 1982

noticed by the European traders. As a result, in principle, no condemned debtors, offenders, or criminals were among the Muslims who landed in the New World."[12] Although in the central Sudan a series of civil wars saw Muslims captured by other Muslims and sold into slavery.

Slavery in the Americas was a vastly different experience than slavery in West Africa. In the New World slavery was linked to skin color not debt, war, crime nor faith. American slavery also dehumanized the slave whereas, in Islamic West Africa, the Quran and Hadith stated that slaves had to be treated with humanity. American slavery was also lifelong and generational. Whereas, manumission was a common practice in Islamic West Africa, in America it was a rare occurrence. For a time in the New World, slavery was a multiracial institution. Europeans, Native Americans, and Africans were all enslaved at some point. Yet, the

---

[12] Diouf, Sylviane A. Servants of Allah: African Muslims Enslaved in the Americas. New York: New York UP, 1998

treatment of European slaves paled in comparison to the treatment endured by others, particularly the African slaves in the New World. "What became unique was that by the sixteenth century Europeans reserved slavery for the Africans and the enslavement of whites totally disappeared."[13] Africans were a cheaper source of slave labor than indentured servants from Europe and it was easier to identify an African slave than it was an European one.

Millions of West Africans were imported into the United States and the Caribbean draining Africa of valuable human capital. These enslaved men and women endured severely harsh treatment from their European enslavers. Forced to work in cotton, tobacco, and rice farms, these men and women were reduced to human chattel, stripped of their culture, and prohibited from practicing their faith. By some

---

[13] Diouf, Sylviane A. Servants of Allah: African Muslims Enslaved in the Americas. New York: New York UP, 1998

estimates, nearly thirty percent of these captured Africans were Muslims. For nearly four hundred years enslaved Africans constituted the sole Muslim population in the Americas.

Arriving in the New World caused many religious challenges for African Muslims. Many European Christian enslavers viewed the religion of Islam as a threat, particularly the Spanish and Portuguese who had been under the rule of Muslim Moors for seven hundred years from 711 AD to 1492 AD. A common tongue of Arabic and a common faith of Islam was a recipe for insurrection, so slave traders went to great lengths to be preemptive. These "pretaliation"[14] tactics included forced conversion to Christianity. Muslims had to adjust their faith practices to fit the confinement of slavery and this meant being creative with their

---

[14] Phrase coined by Dr. Michael Eric Dyson. It implies conducting unprovoked aggressive action based on the idea that one might be attacked in the future.

practice of Islam even at times camouflaging their faith and wearing a "mask that grins and lies". They maintained the will to practice their faith but also had to contend with the realities of their enslavement. Some would publicly convert to Christianity but secretly practice Islam. Others would openly maintain their commitment to the Five Pillars. Regardless of the adaptation, many enslaved African Muslims maintained dedication and fidelity to Islam.

These stories of Islamic perseverance can best be exampled by the life of Abd-Al-Rahman Ibrahima. His story was first captured in a pamphlet titled "A Statement with Regard to the Moorish Prince, Abduhl Rahhahman" by Thomas H. Gallaudet. He was called "The Prince" because he was born the son of the King of Sori in Guinea 1762. He attended school in Timbuktu where he learned to read and write Arabic. According to Gallaudet, when Ibrahima was nineteen years old his homeland was visited by Dr. John Cox an American surgeon. Cox was on a hunting mission and fell ill. He was nursed to health in Ibrahima's kingdom and shown great hospitality by the people. During his six-month stay, Cox became friends with Ibrahima.

In Ibrahima's adulthood, a war developed between ethnic groups in his homeland. The conflict started when the Jalunke, an ethnic tribe, announced that public prayer was outlawed. This was considered an affront and an attack on Muslims and a cause for the Muslim cleric Fulbe to declare war. Ibrahima was a young military leader within the army and fought for the cause of Islam. He was ambushed and captured and sold to the Mandingos. Later he was sold to European slave traders and placed aboard a ship headed to the New World. His journey ended in Natchez Mississippi where he was bought by a man named Colonel Thomas Foster. For nearly two decades, he worked as a slave for Col. Foster. Abd-Al-Rahman Ibrahima, the former prince, had been reduced to a field hand.

This was his reality until one fateful day while selling in a market, Ibrahima was spotted by an old friend, Dr. Cox. Taken aback by the prince's condition and remembering the hospitality shown to him, Cox was moved to request manumission for Ibrahima from Col. Foster. His request was denied.

Dr. Cox died in 1816 and his son took up the cause of manumission for another decade. In 1826 a letter that Ibrahima wrote was given to United States Senator Thomas Reed. Reed, assuming Ibrahima to be a Moor because the letter was written in Arabic, forwarded the letter to the Moroccan Consulate. His letter eventually reached the Sultan of Morocco, Abderramane, who petitioned President John Quincy Adams for the release of Ibrahima. In 1828 the United States Secretary of State, Henry Clay secured the manumission of Ibrahima.

Ibrahima became famous throughout the country. The story of the "Moroccan Prince" forced into slavery spread and intrigued many Americans. Hundreds of people would gather to him speak of his experience. He used this fame to raise money in an attempt to buy the freedom of his wife and children. He traveled the country telling his story under the moniker "the Prince". He was able to raise enough money to free his wife but not enough to obtain the freedom of his children. He returned to Africa in 1828 after a forty year sojourn and died one year later in Monrovia Liberia.

In Ibrahima's story, there is also an example of how some enslaved Muslims adjusted faith to their new context. Gallaudet wrote of Ibrahima "since his residence in this country, Prince has embraced the Christian religion. Himself, wife and eldest son have been baptized, and are in connection with the Baptist church."[15] Yet, when he was asked to prove his Christianity by writing the Lord Prayer, Ibrahima resourcefully wrote the opening surah of the Quran, Al- Fatiha.

Isolation in small communities often benefitted the enslaved Muslims that attempted to maintain their faith. Sapelo and St. Simons Islands, off the coast of Georgia, are examples of this benefit of isolation. "Both Sapelo and St. Simons are a part of the Gullah-Geechee Heritage Corridor. The Gullah-Geechee are descendants of West African slaves who lived on islands and in mainland communities stretching from North Carolina to northern Florida near Jacksonville. Their isolation allowed them to retain their West African traditions."[16]

---

[15] Gallaudet, T. H. A statement with regard to the Moorish prince Abduhl Rahhahman. New York: appointed to solicit Subscriptions in New York to aid redeeming the Family of the Prince from Slavery, 1828.

[16] "Muslims in Early Georgia: Introduction." Http://libguides.ccga.edu/muslims. College of Coastal Georgia Libraries, 20 June 2016.

Bismillah and Bean Pies

Bilali Muhammad was one of the enslaved Muslims on Sapelo Island. Muhammad was born in the city of Timbo, in what is presently Guinea, in 1770. He was educated in his homeland and was fluent in Arabic. He was, at some point, captured and sold into slavery and eventually sold to a plantation owner on Sapelo Island. Because of the isolation of the island and possibly because of a less strict owner, Thomas Spalding, Muhammad was able to practice his faith openly. Because of his education and literacy Muhammad rose to a leadership position on the plantation. But, his greatest accomplishment was not in labor management but in Islamic jurisprudence. Muhammad, quite possibly, wrote the first book of Islamic law written in the United States. "This is evidenced by a thirteen-page manuscript he wrote and gifted to a southern writer, Francis Robert Goulding before he died in 1857. The manuscript was written in Arabic and was thus unreadable for most Americans for decades. It made its way eventually to the Georgia State Library by 1931, who attempted to decipher the manuscript, which was popularly believed to have been Bilali's diary."[17] What Muhammad had written was not at all a diary, it was "a copy of passages from a treatise on Islamic Law in the Maliki madhab written by a Muslim scholar of fiqh, Ibn Abu Zayd al-Qairawani in Tunisia in the 900s. The Risala of Ibn Abu Zayd was a part of the West African law curriculum prevalent in Bilali's homeland in the 1700s when he was a student."[18] Muhammad had memorized these passages of law years before and had written them down in Arabic. This is an example of the extent enslaved Muslims had to go to preserve their faith.

---

[17] Alkhateeb, Firas. "The First Muslim-American Scholar: Bilali Muhammad." Lost Islamic History. Web. <lostislamichistory.com> 24 Feb 2014.

[18] Alkhateeb, Firas. "The First Muslim-American Scholar: Bilali Muhammad." Lost Islamic History. Web. <lostislamichistory.com> 24 Feb 2014.

There was an empty lot located at 3324 Dent Place in Old Georgetown, an upscale neighborhood in Washington, DC, that once housed another African American Muslim of note. That man was Yarrow Mamout. Mamout was born in Guinea. He was educated and literate in Arabic. It is believed that he was captured and enslaved at sixteen in 1752. He gained his freedom at the age of sixty after more than forty years as a slave.

His story then takes a unique turn. "Mamout as a brick maker who earned top dollar for his work and "a jack of all trades" who made money making charcoal, loading ships and weaving baskets. He earned enough not only to acquire the Dent Place property but also to become a financier who lent money to merchants. He owned stock in the Columbia Bank of Georgetown."[19]

---

[19] King, Colbert. "Yarrow Mamout, the slave who became a Georgetown financier." The Washington Post. Web. <washingtonpost.com/opinions/yarrow-mamout>

Bismillah and Bean Pies

Mamout purchased the property and lived there until his death. He was known to pray facing Mecca, abstaining from pork, and alcohol. His investment in the bank allowed him to purchase the freedom of one of his sons and even lend money to entrepreneurs in the Washington, DC area. It was this business that brought him to the attention of the artist Charles Wilson Peale. "The artist was hobnobbing with presidents, politicians, scientists, philosophers, and the rich and famous when he heard of the African. That such a great man wanted to paint a former slave made a big impression on Yarrow, and Yarrow made a lasting impression on Peale as well."[20] Mamout was painted wearing a kufi and traditional Muslim beard. Mamout is another example of how enslaved African Muslims held on to their faith in the New World.

---

[20] Johnston, John H. From Slave Ship to Harvard: Yarrow Mamout and the History of an African American Family. New York: Fordham University Press, 2010

Bismillah and Bean Pies

These are just a few examples how enslaved African Muslims were able to maintain their faith by making adaptations in the new American context. Holding on to their Islamic faith, though challenging, was possible for first-generation African Muslims in the New World. This cannot be said for their children, who were often reared in the faith of their European masters. For these second and subsequent generations, Africa was a concept not a memory and Islam all but disappeared.

Bismillah and Bean Pies

Chapter Two: Marcus, Muslims, and
Missionaries

Bismillah and Bean Pies

In 1807, the United States Congress abolished the importation of slaves. The act prohibited the import of "slaves into any port or place within the jurisdiction of the United States from any foreign kingdom, place, or country." These words effectively severed enslaved Africans in the New World from any bond to Africa and erased many African cultural practices including the practice of Islam. Without the import of new Africans into the system there was no connectivity to West Africa and Islam. Africans born in the New World, particularly in the United States, were made Christians and there was virtually no mention of Islam in subsequent generations. Even through a systematic attempt to erase the African's identity traditions including Islam were secreted and shared.

Still, Islam became as foreign to second generation Africans as the New World was to their parents. It was not until a man from the Virgin Islands discovers Islam while living in West Africa, that the faith would have a re-genesis in Black America. That man was Edward Wilmot Blyden. Bylden is credited with being the father of "Pan-Africanism" and it was through this prism that he proposed Islam as a liberating faith for Africans worldwide.

Blyden was born in St. Thomas to an educated family in 1832. His family later moved to Venezuela from 1842 to 1844, where Blyden learned Spanish. He later returned to St. Thomas to continue his education. An American missionary pastor named John P. Knox took note of Blyden's intelligence and mentored him in the Christian faith. Knox later encouraged Blyden to seek education in the United States at Rutgers Theological College. He arrived in the United States in 1850 and attempted to enroll in the school but he was denied because of his race. That year, the Fugitive Slave Act of 1850 became law and was heavily enforced. This law gave leeway for freemen to be captured or recaptured and forced into slavery. It was viewed as a threat to every black person in the United States as it required law enforcement to capture "fugitive slaves" with little evidence of their fugitive status. "As a result, more and more prominent African-American intellectuals, including the Harvard-trained physician Martin Delany, began to advocate black emigration from the United States. While Delany promoted Latin America and the Caribbean as potential sites for black settlement, Edward Blyden spoke early on in favor of Africa."[21] Blyden decided it was not safe for him to stay in the United States because he feared being forced into slavery. With the help of a Presbyterian pastor, Blyden immigrated to Liberia, West Africa.

Upon arriving in Liberia, Blyden enrolled in Alexander High School in Monrovia. At Alexander, he studied Hebrew and continued his embrace of the Christian faith. He was later ordained a Presbyterian

---

[21] Curtis, Edward E. Islam in Black America: identity, liberation, and difference in African-American Islamic thought. New York: State University of New York Press, 2002

minister in 1858. He eventually became the principal of Alexander High School a position that earned him high esteem. Blyden was well-educated, multilingual and ambitious and these traits helped to raise his public profile in the country of Liberia. He was at once a scholar, theologian, and linguist. In 1862 he became a professor at the University of Liberia and started to study Arabic. Two years later he was chosen to be secretary of state of Liberia. It was in this position that afforded him the opportunity to participate in official state missions particularly in the Islamic kingdoms in the interior of West Africa. He was able to witness the liberating narrative of Islam firsthand and experience the communal aspects of the faith.

Blyden was briefly exiled from 1871-1873 in Sierra Leone. While in exile, he wrote and traveled. After a brief return to Liberia and a failed bid for the presidency of the country, Blyden returned to Sierra Leone. It was at this time that Blyden loosened his embrace of Christianity and studied Islam extensively. Blyden eventually became Director of Muslim Education in Sierra Leone and in this capacity he started promoting the idea that Islam was a more natural religion for black people worldwide. Blyden became a critic of Christianity and the missionaries that were being sent into Africa. These missionaries often came to Africa with a cultural bias that was both detrimental and offensive to native cultures. "Cultural contact is a two-way affair and the meeting of two civilizations, European and African, was also a two-way process. The attitudes of Europeans towards Africa and the Africans in this period of cultural contact can be better understood only if they are seen as a part of a wider intellectual system, a total world view. This world view, which Europeans derived from contemplating their own European societies and on which European cultural tradition was based, served to distort and tint the cultural filters through which Europeans observed

Bismillah and Bean Pies

other parts of the world, and especially Africa."[22] Europeans took it as their duty to "civilize" the other races of the world and spread the faith of Christianity. The duty of "civilizing" could not be separated from ideas of white supremacy thus limiting the Europeans intellectual ability to engage with Africans with reciprocity and respect. Blyden viewed the Christian religion and the missionaries that propagated the faith as weapons used to reduce Africans into servitude. Blyden stated, "whenever the Negro is found in Christian lands, his leading trait is not docility, as has been often alleged, but servility." He also became a critic of black Americans that accepted second class citizenship and had not built a separate nation of their own. He wrote ""I would rather go naked and wander among the natives of the interior (of Africa) than occupy the

---

[22] Pawlikova-Vilhanova, Viera Christianity, Islam and the African world: Edward Wilmot Blyden(1832-1912) and contemporary missionary thought. Institute of Oriental and African Studies, Slovak Academy of Sciences, 2002 pg 117-128

position of some of the respectable colored people in the U.S., for then I should feel that I was in a country of my own."

Blyden's book "Christianity, Islam and the Negro Race" is considered the first time that Islam and black nationalism coalesced and was critically examined as a viable option to unify Africans worldwide. He developed the framework that viewed Islam through the prism of pan-Africanism and Black Nationalism and his genetics can be seen in every expression of African American Islam from the Moorish Science Temple to the community of Imam WD Muhammad. In his book, "Blyden was highly sympathetic to Islam in Africa. Comparing it with Christianity he praised it as a unifying factor cutting across ethnic lines and having an elevating influence by bringing the Arabic language and literature to

Africans."[23] He believed that Islam's lack of imagery of Allah(God) and the prophets democratized Islam in a way that Christianity couldn't because of Christianity's use of Eurocentric images of Jesus, prophets, and other figures. In short, Christianity made the divine white which created, in Blydens opinion, a demoralizing and debilitating effect on the psyche and esteem of African people. He promoted the ideas of Africans being the messiahs of the world and through Africans, the world might be redeemed.

Blyden viewed racial separation as key to changing the condition of Africans worldwide and that Islam was the vehicle that could facilitate the building of a black nation. "He argued that separation of the races into separate nations was essential to racial equality. "We shall

---

[23] Pawlikova-Vilhanova, Viera Christianity, Islam and the African world: Edward Wilmot Blyden(1832-1912) and contemporary missionary thought. Institute of Oriental and African Studies, Slovak Academy of Sciences, 2002 pg 117-128

never receive," he wrote, "the respect of other races until we establish a powerful nationality." Moreover, Blyden said,"the heart of every true Negro yearns after a distinct and separate nationality."[24] Blyden viewed Islam as the cultural foundation on which African nationality should be erected. It was Islamic African societies, he argued, that had produced the greatest examples of African accomplishments. He viewed these Muslim societies as producing Africans with dignity, pride, and a sense of accomplishment. "Blyden's ultimate goal was the vindication of the African race. In seeking to oppose current racist theories he developed his own concept of race, stressing the virtues of the African race and fostering pride in its history and culture. The basic concept of Blyden's works was a successful endeavor to interpret the history and culture of Africa from the point of view of

---

[24] Curtis, Edward E. Islam in Black America: identity, liberation, and difference in African-American Islamic thought. New York: State University of New York Press, 2002

Bismillah and Bean Pies

Africans themselves. Blyden continually had in mind the future of Africa and the Africans, but saw it always in terms of historical continuity."[25]

He married this view of Islam with an idea of Black Nationalism. He wrote "we must build up Negro states; we must establish and maintain the institutions; we must make and administer laws, erect and preserve churches, and support the worship of God; we must have governments; we must have legislation of our own; we must build ships and navigate them; we must ply the trades, instruct the schools, control the press, and thus aid in shaping and guiding the destinies of

---

[25] Pawlikova-Vilhanova, Viera Christianity, Islam and the African world: Edward Wilmot Blyden(1832-1912) and contemporary missionary thought. Institute of Oriental and African Studies, Slovak Academy of Sciences, 2002 pg 117-128

mankind."[26] Again, Blyden's writings set the intellectual framework for the idea of Black Nationalism. His writings birth the consciousness that raised black nationalist leaders including Marcus Garvey who, probably more than any other, sought to establish Blyden's ideas of black nationhood.

Marcus Garvey was the Moses of the African Diaspora organizing to lead his people out of 'Egypt' into the promised land. If Blyden's writings were the intellectual framework for Black Nationalism, then Garvey's work was the brick masonry around that frame. Garvey was very likely influenced by Blyden through the writings of J.E.Casely Hayford. Hayford was a student of Blyden and authored a very important piece of Pan-African literature entitled Ethiopia Unbound. Duse Muhammad Ali was also a student of Blyden and a mentor to Garvey. Ali, more than any

---

[26] Curtis, Edward E. Islam in Black America: identity, liberation, and difference in African-American Islamic thought. New York: State University of New York Press, 2002

other, influenced Garvey's philosophical view of the African Diaspora. Garvey, unlike any before him, progressed the idea of Black Nationalism in the minds of Africans throughout the United States and the Caribbean. His teachings and organization laid the groundwork for every Black Nationalist organization that came after. Like Blyden, Garvey's influence can be seen in the work of the Moorish Science Temple, the Nation of Islam, the Black Panther Party, the work of Martin Luther King and the Southern Christian Leadership Council, and the Rastafarian religion. Garvey's Universal Negro Improvement Association (UNIA) may have had membership in the millions yet regardless of the enrollment in the organization, the UNIA, and Garvey influenced the consciousness of all of Black America and brought to the forefront the idea of Black Nationalism.

Garvey was born in Jamaica. He was the youngest of eleven children and his father Marcus

Bismillah and Bean Pies

Garvey, Sr., was influential in making the younger Garvey have a love for reading and learning. Garvey was mainly self-taught, besides a stint at the University of London, yet he was well read, a skill that would later come to benefit him as a newspaper editor. At fourteen, Garvey became a printer's apprentice and moved to Kingston, Jamaica.

At only twenty years old, Garvey became involved in a printer strike and though the effort was ultimately unsuccessful, it helped Garvey to develop an interest in activism. He worked on behalf of migrant workers in Central America before leaving for London. In London Garvey came under the tutelage of Duse Muhammad Ali. Ali was a Muslim, an African Nationalist and the owner of the African Times and Orient Review. Ali used the paper as a way of promoting Islam and the ideas of nationalism. "Ali was one of the most important and colorful figures in the global pan-Africanist movement. Although he lived in London he exercised a strong influence on the black nationalist movement in the United States, particularly on Marcus Garvey."[27] Ali was the son of an Egyptian father and a Sudanese mother. Garvey was greatly influenced by Ali and his brand of African Islamic Nationalism. "Duse's influence on Garvey is attested to by his wife, Amy Jacques Garvey, and can be seen in the UNIA's motto of 'One God, One Aim, One Destiny' and in various Islamically inspired anthems of the organization."[28]

Garvey returned to Jamaica and founded the UNIA with an expressed goal of uniting the Africa Diaspora and establishing an independent nation. His correspondence with African American educator, Booker T. Washington, lead Garvey to the

---

[27] Haddad, Yvonne Y. Esposito, John L. Muslims on the Americanization Path?. New York: Oxford University Press

[28] Haddad, Yvonne Y. Smith, Jane I. Muslim Minorities in the West. Oxford: Altamira Press, 2002

Bismillah and Bean Pies

United States. He settled in New York City and started to spread his message of Black Nationalism through his Negro World newspaper. By 1919 Garvey founded a shipping company, the Black Star Line, to establish trade with blacks in the Caribbean, Africa, and the United States. In just one year, Garvey claimed a membership in the millions and held a convention that drew twenty-five thousand people. Garvey had the gift of oratory flair that attracted thousands of people. "Garvey was a dramatic speaker who idealized the black race and its homeland in Africa."[29]

His businesses were less successful than his organizational building and soon his ventures folded. The FBI under the leadership of J. Edgar Hoover, targeted the UNIA for investigation and Garvey was arrested. In 1923 he was convicted of mail fraud imprisoned and in 1927 deported to Jamaica.

---

[29] Turner, Richard Brent Islam in the African American Experience . Indiana: Indiana University Press 1997, 2003

Bismillah and Bean Pies

Garvey told reporters, while in prion, that his conviction was a "result of efforts of my opponents of the colored race. They are light-colored Negroes who think that the Negro can always develop in this country. They also resent the fact that I, a black Negro, am a leader."[30]

Although his stay in the United States was a mere five years before his conviction, his influence was far reaching and wide ranging. "As UNIA activist Samuel Haynes wrote in the 14 January 1928 issue of the Negro World, 'Garvey, living or dead, is our patron saint, our supreme leader, and counsellor, and neither the cannon of hate nor the whip of prejudice can swerve us from our allegiance to him and the great ideal of African nationalism.'"[31] Although his sojourn in the United States was

---

[30] Evanzz, Karl The Messenger: the rise and fall of Elijah Muhmmad. New York: Random House, 1999

[31] Hill, Robert A and Garvey, Marcus The Marcus Garvey and Universal Negro Improvement Association Papers. California: University of California Press, 1991

aborted, by the time Garvey was deported the country was very different from when he first arrived in the United States. The UNIA faced internal challenges that left the organization fractured and financially suffering. The membership base dwindled as other organizations arose with Garvey-esque leaders.

"Given the failure of Garvey's emigration plans to get off of dry land, it was fortunate that the UNIA's appeal was broad-based. Certainly, the organization's stated aims and objectives offered something for everyone. As initially outlined, they were "to establish a Universal Confraternity among the race; to promote the spirit of pride and love; to reclaim the fallen; to administer to and assist the needy; to assist in civilizing the backwards tribes of Africa; to assist in the development of Independent Negro nations and communities."[32] Garvey's ideas of Black Nationalism, shaped by Pan-Africanism, inspired millions even through the midst of Garvey's business and legal troubles.

Garvey was received in Jamaica by massive crowds of people. He was the black "messiah" arisen after his prison stint. He took to the lecture circuit with hopes of reinvigorating his followers. His philosophy now shaped and influenced by "London-a hotbed of Pan-Africanism and by Islam, the unifying religion of many African and Asian intellectuals."[33] He faced difficulties including being denied admission to Costa Rica to give a speech. Yet, his speeches were still magnetic and powerful. He was masterful with words and rhetoric, traits that are often found in many

---

[32] Van Deburg, William L. Modern Black Nationalism: From Marcus Garvey to Louis Farrakhan. New York: New York University Press, 1997

[33] Turner, Richard Brent Islam in the African American Experience . Indiana: Indiana University Press 1997, 2003

Black Nationalist leaders. "Garvey's speeches throughout the late 1920s are evidence of the renewed dynamism he felt emerging from a period of involuntary activity. They reflect strong religious and metaphysical beliefs, revealing him to be even more of a proponent of optimistic New Thought philosophy than he had been in the past."[34]

    The UNIA set the perimeters of nationalism by creating retail businesses within the black community, including factories, laundries, and restaurants. Furthermore, Garvey introduced the idea of a religion specific to the black people of the world. "Religious nationalist undoubtedly were pleased to learn that many Garveyites worshiped a 'Black Man of Sorrows' and had their own Universal Negro Catechism and Universal Negro Ritual. Here, black nationalism was seen as the fulfillment of prophecy

---

[34] Hill, Robert A and Garvey, Marcus The Marcus Garvey and Universal Negro Improvement Association Papers. California: University of California Press, 1991

and Garvey apotheosized as the 'reincarnated Angel of Peace come from Heaven to dispense Political Salvation' to an oppressed people.[35] The power of the Garvey's movement was its ability to bridge nationality, religion, and Pan-Africanism. "Although Marcus Garvey was a Roman Catholic convert and his followers were predominantly Christians, this did not pose a problem for Muslims, who were attracted to the UNIA because of its multidimensional religious orientation. Indeed, Randall Burkett has argued convincingly that Garvey intended to establish a black civil religion with an ethos and a worldview drawn from the tradition of the black church yet charged with self-consciousness of black nationalism."[36] Garvey understood the importance of religion to African

---

[35] Van Deburg, William L. Modern Black Nationalism: From Marcus Garvey to Louis Farrakhan. New York: New York University Press, 1997

[36] Turner, Richard Brent Islam in the African American Experience. Indiana: Indiana University Press 1997, 2003

people and tailored not only a political movement but also a (re)visioning of religious thought. His idea of creating a specifically black religion and rejection of Eurocentric Christianity was likely influenced by Ethiopia Unbound in which the white church was viewed as racist and unfit for Africans.

"Although his alternative programs were not always successful, Garvey's rhetoric and public image inspired and attracted Muslim leaders who had the same goals. Drew Ali, Mufti Muhammad Sadiq, and Elijah Muhammad were all politically connected to Garveyism in different ways and mentioned Garvey frequently in their speeches and writings"[37] Garvey's mentor, Duse Muhammad Ali, worked for the UNIA in the 1920s writing for the Negro World. Ali would later found the Universal Islamic Society in Detroit in 1926 which mirrored in many ways the structural design of

---

[37] Turner, Richard Brent Islam in the African American Experience. Indiana: Indiana University Press 1997, 2003

the UNIA with an Islamic specification. The UNIA became the framework for how Islam would be (re)presented in the new African American context. Muslim leaders learned from Garvey's massive influence and understood what attracted his followers and implemented those tactics into their own movements. Blyden's ideas of nationalism based on Islamic principles influenced Garvey and now Garvey was inspiring Islamic movements in the Black America. This opportunity was sieged upon by a group of Muslims, in 1922, that attempted to persuade Garvey to establish Islam as the official religion of the UNIA. Although the proposal was rejected, Garvey started to incorporate Islamic themes into his speeches and writings. Garvey is quoted in a speech as saying, "Muhammad suffered many defeats at certain times but Muhammad stuck to his faith and ultimately triumphed and Muhammedanism was given to the world. And as Muhammad did in the religious world, so in the political arena we have had men who have paid the price for leading the people toward the great light of liberty." In the Negro World Garvey was compared to Prophet Muhammad and another writer called Garvey "a child of Allah." The incorporation of Islam into the UNIA also included the musical director, Arnold Ford, who composed hymns that included Islamic themes such as one entitled "Allah-Hu-Akbar" and another with the lyrics "may he our rights proclaim, in that most sacred name Allah."

Garvey and the UNIA's embrace of Islamic principles and symbols assisted in redefining black American religious expression. The stronghold of Christianity was loosened and the idea of an alternative belief system became at least palatable to the black masses in tuned with Garvey's movement. Garvey never became a Muslim and most likely only viewed the faith as a means to a political end nevertheless, his inclusion of the faith left fertile ground for other Islamic organizations to plant seeds and grow the faith. Garvey "as a non-Muslim, exposed more socially conscious blacks to Islamic ideas than the tens of thousands of Muslim immigrants residing in the West at that time."[38] His influence is obvious in the economic programs of Noble Drew Ali's Moorish Science Temple and the Nation of Islam as well as their promotion of the ideas self-sufficiency and self-reliance. "Drew Ali cast him as John the Baptist to his Jesus: 'In these modern days there came a forerunner of Jesus, who was divinely prepared by the great God-Allah and his name is Marcus Garvey, who did teach and warn the nations of the earth to prepare to meet the coming Prophet.'"[39] Elijah Muhammad called both Noble Drew Ali and Marcus Garvey Muslims and felt that he was the inheritor of their brand of black

---

[38] Haddad, Yvonne Y. Smith, Jane I. Muslim Minorities in the West. Oxford: Altamira Press, 2002

[39] Berg, Herbert Elijah Muhammad and Islam. New York: New York University Press, 2009

Islamic nationalism. He is quoted as stating "Both of these men were fine Muslims. The followers of Noble Drew Ali and Marcus Garvey should now follow me and cooperate with us in our work because we are only trying to finish up what those before us started."[40]

The Islamic traditions that were affiliated with Garvey and later developed into ideological offspring of the UNIA, developed almost independently of immigrant Muslims communities that arrived in the United States starting in 1875. This may have been in part to the stronghold Christianity had on African Americans and the unavailability of Quran's and Islamic literature. Nevertheless, Muslim immigrants did not establish any significant relationships with African Americans nor is there much evidence to suggests any attempt to introduce Islam to black communities except for the Ahmadiyya Muslim community and

---

[40] Berg, Herbert Elijah Muhammad and Islam. New York: New York University Press, 2009

Universal Islamic Society both of which had ties to Garvey and the UNIA. "The Ahmadiyya movement, the Islamic Mission of America, and the Universal Islamic Society made efforts to inculcate Black America with Islam in the mid-1920s."[41]

The Ahmadiyya Muslim Community was founded in India by Mirza Ghulam Ahmad. Ahmad came from a prominent family and gained popularity as an Islamic writer who authored over ninety books. Around the age of forty Ahmad claimed that God communicated with him and inspired him to revive Islam. Ahmad later claimed to be the messiah and the Mahdi and traveled his homeland teaching, writing, and debating. He drew criticism from Islamic and Christian communities for his teachings. The Ahmadi are called unbelievers or heretics by many Sunni Muslims. The Ahmadi are given these labels based on Ahmad's innovations.His teaching are

---

[41] Gibson, Dawn-Marie A History of the Nation of Islam: Race, Islam, and the Quest for Freedom. California: ABC-CLIO, 2012

considered, by Sunni Muslims, to be un-Islamic. It is important to note some of the controversial teachings of Ahmad are similar to the teachings of some black Islamic organizations. The Ahmadi believe that the messiah and Mahdi are the same being. This is distinctly different from the Sunni belief of Jesus being the Messiah and will return in the physical form and the Mahdi is the 12th imam that is to come with Jesus. The Ahmadi believe that the Quran is the final revelation of Allah but they also believe that Allah continues to communicate with humankind through people. They accept the idea that new prophets can come but they will come as Muslims to reform or revive the faith. Lastly, Ahmadi Muslims believe no verse in the Quran cancels another. These, along with the claim of Ahmad to be both the messiah and Mahdi, separated the Ahmadi from much of the Sunni Islamic world. It is possible that this disconnect from the rest of the Islamic community fueled the Ahmadi's desire to propagate Islam in the United States and eventually to focus specifically on African Americans.

In the beginning of the twentieth century, the Ahmadiyya Muslim Community influenced many African Americans and actively sought them as converts. "The missionaries set up a series of mosques on the East coast and in the Midwest, all of which were identified by the preface 'the First Mosque.'"[42] Study groups (this term will later be used by the Nation of Islam) were established to teach basic tenants of Islam to new converts. The Moslem Sunrise(an English language Muslim newspaper) was established, much like the UNIA's Negro World, to spread the organization's message.

The Ahmadi sent Mufti Muhammad Sadiq to the United States as a missionary in 1920. Sadiq found great opposition to Islam with white Anglo-Saxon Protestants and started to focus his efforts on converting African Americans, who

---

[42] McCloud, Aminah Beverly African American Islam. New York: Routledge, 1995

appeared to be more open to the faith.

Dr. Fatima Fanusie suggests that Ahmadiyya intellectuals proposed spreading Islam in Black America similarly to the way it was spread in India. "Ahmadiyya Muslims similarly emphasized in their writings how medieval era Sufi Saints and Muslim mystics had converted illiterate Hindu peasants to a nominally Islamic identity by juxtaposing Islamic names and events over Hindu names and celebrations in a process where a true Islamic identity actually took centuries to unfold."[43] Fanuise suggests that a later manifestation of this type of Islamic particularism can be seen in the formation of Nation of Islam about a decade after Sadiq's mission.

Sadiq set up a mission on Chicago's South-side and begin to tailor his Ahmadi beliefs to fit the

---

[43] Fanusie, Fatima "Fard Muhmmad in Historic Context" Lecture Georgetown University March 26, 2014

concerns and conditions of African American migrants arriving in Chicago from the Deep South due to the end of slavery. Sadiq presented Islam as the stolen legacy of African Americans ripped from them when the "Christian profiteers brought you out of your native lands of Africa and in Christianizing you made you forget the religion and language of your forefathers-which were Islam and Arabic."[44] Sadiq believed and promoted the idea of equality for all men including African Americans. This idea was virtually unheard of in the white Christians teachings to which most of the migrants had been exposed. The Ahmadi newspaper, the Moslem Sunrise, wrote articles critical of racism, particularly in the Christian church. In a context in which one of the most famous "Christian" organization was the Ku Klux Klan, the Moslem Sunrise's claim of racism in the Christian church was easy to prove. The

---

[44] Curtis, Edwards E. Islamism and its African American Muslim Critics: Black Muslims in the Era of the Arab Cold War. American Quarterly Journal 2007

Bismillah and Bean Pies

Moslem Sunrise declared to Black Americans "You need a religion," the article declared, "which teaches manliness, self-reliance, self-respect, and self-effort." Sadiq was successful in directly converting one thousand Americans, mainly African Americans, to Islam. He returned to India in 1923.

Another Ahmadiyya community was established by Wali Akram in Cleveland, Ohio. He built a following of two hundred people from 1934 through 1940. His community was not only one of religion but also finance and Akram envisioned a "ten-year plan" for the community.

The Ahmadi's most important contribution to the spread of Islam in the African American community was the making available of an English translation of the Quran. "Ahmadi developed and circulated most of the literature available to African-American Muslims for decades, including copies of the

Quran."[45] The Quran translation the Ahmadi distributed was the Mawlana Muhammad Ali translation which was also the same translation given to Elijah Muhammad by his teacher Fard Muhammad. "The membership of the Ahmadiyya movement in America during the years 1917-1960 was predominately African American"[46] which assisted with reconfiguring the African American religious landscape.

Because of the rigors of the religion, including the five daily prayers and Jummah pray on Fridays, many African Americans in Ahmadiyya community became merchants which permitted them the opportunity practice their faith without limitations of work schedule. This trait is still evident in African American Muslim communities.

---

[45] Gibson, Dawn-Marie A History of the Nation of Islam: Race, Islam, and the Quest for Freedom. California: ABC-CLIO, 2012

[46] McCloud, Aminah Beverly African American Islam. New York: Routledge, 1995

The budding community started to face difficulty. "Dissension arose due to the fact that African Americans were never appointed as missionaries. The title of shakyh acknowledged their accomplishments in Islamic studies but did not give them any authority over the communities...Original members insisted on Indian customs and interpretations, rather than seeing African American culture as having something to offer American Islam."[47] The substitute supremacy of the Ahmadi necessitated an independent black expression of Islam, one that was reflective of the experience and cultural context in which Black America was emerging.

In 1924 the son of a Moroccan father and a Jamaican mother organized what became known as the Islamic Mission of America. Shaykh(Sheikh) Dauod Ahmed Faisal organization was the first explicitly black Sunni Islamic organization. Faisal organization was

---

[47] McCloud, Aminah Beverly African American Islam. New York: Routledge, 1995

not nationalist in inception or ideology. "Whereas the Moorish Science Temple community resisted attempts by the United States government to draft its men into the armed forces the Islamic Mission of America permitted its male followers to join...Faisal thought that blacks should reclaim their Islamic heritage and also lay claim to an American allegiance."[48] This type of "duel citizenship" will later be promoted by Imam WD Muhammad. Faisal invited Muslims from all backgrounds to his masjid including immigrant Muslims. He sought to unify the numerous Muslim communities of the East coast and act as a central Islamic authority. According to Beverly McCloud, author of African American Islam, Faisal was responsible for converting over sixty Americans to Islam in his lifetime.

Faisal sought to connect the fledgling American Muslim communities with the rest of the Muslim world. He formed alliances

---

[48] McCloud, Aminah Beverly African American Islam. New York: Routledge, 1995

with Muslim seamen that docked in New York harbor and offered them a place to make salaat(prayers) and other benefits associated with being a member of an Islamic community including a Salat al Janazah the Islamic funeral prayer. Like the Ahmadi, the Islamic Mission of America also distributed literature and eventually the Yusuf Ali English translation of the Quran. Faisal often used materials from other Muslim missionaries including the Ahmadi and at one point distributed the Ahmadi's English translation of the Quran.

Faisal promoted the universal brotherhood of Islam and believed it to be the one true religion that could unify and bring peace to humanity. Although, he expressed Islam's universal teachings, he was highly critical of Judaism and Christianity particularly the explicit racism in the expression of those faiths in the United States. He believed that Jews would not accept a man of color into their community and would resist that person as if he were a murderer.

He said of Christianity that it was a "social order, a philosophy based on certain principles of White Supremacy."[49] Faisal's perception of Judaism and Christianity was probably a result of traditional Islamic rhetoric and the racism he may have experienced in the United States, nevertheless, Faisal movement was not race centered and sought to be compliant with the American social order. "In fact, some of his followers left the Islamic Mission precisely because they believed Shaikh Daoud to be overly supportive of the political status quo."[50] This splinter group would become known as Darul Islam. The Darul Islamic community expressed a stricter adherence to the faith. This community would later advocate prohibition against association with

---

[49] Curtis, Edwards E. Islamism and its African American Muslim Critics: Black Muslims in the Era of the Arab Cold War. American Quarterly Journal 2007

[50] Curtis, Edwards E. Islamism and its African American Muslim Critics: Black Muslims in the Era of the Arab Cold War. American Quarterly Journal 2007

non-Muslims. The group later split again and other organizations were formed including the twenty masjids headed by Jamil al Amin(H. Rap Brown).

The context in which Islam emerges within Black America is one veneered with nationalism, resistance to racism, and a rejection of Christianity. These elements combined to create an Islamic protest religion that is draped in political consciousness and that is uniquely and keenly aware of race. This expression uses the faith of Islam as a liberating and unifying mechanism that challenges white supremacy, Christian racism, and American morality. Islam and Black Nationalism have become inextricably linked forming equipoise and symmetry that distinguishes this expression from any other Islamic articulation. It is an expression based on the experience of African Americans and transmissive of their desires for liberation. Early Black Islamic communities were as equally religious organizations as they were political and social movements which rallied against structural racism and white supremacy as much as they rallied against Shatan and the perils of sin.

Bismillah and Bean Pies

Chapter Three: Particularism, Moorish Science, and the Nation of Islam

Bismillah and Bean Pies

Edward E. Curtis, the author of several works on Islam in Black America, theorizes the idea of "black particularism" in Islam. The idea is in contrast to universalism or the belief that Islam is an all-encompassing faith that has eliminated the need for an individual prescription, particularism, for different groups of adherents. Universalism suggests that Islam in Pakistan and Islam in Detroit should be expressed and experienced identically in ritual and practice, by these very different groups of Muslims. The idea of universalism, at times, is far too simplistic and insufficient to address the unique concerns of over a billion adherents. At the genesis of African-American Islamic thought a challenge was presented: "How do African-Americans create an Islamic expression that is both relevant to the black experience and true to the core tenants of Islam?" "Many times, this debate becomes one over the question of what exactly constitutes 'identity and culture' versus what constitutes proper Islamic belief and observance."[51] In the greater Islamic world, faith, nationalism, and culture are often intertwined which further complicates African-American Muslims ability to determine authentic Islamic ideology as they observe these different communities and attempt to emerge from centuries of religious hibernation to reconnect with the greater Islamic world. These concerns coupled with the experience of racism and prejudice from white society and immigrant Muslim populations make it difficult to see an embrace of universalism by African-American Muslims. "And yet they have done so from the very beginning of their history as Muslim converts: African-American Islamic universalism has been a remarkably idealistic expression of the hope for human

---

[51] Curtis, Edward E. Islam in Black America: identity, liberation, and difference in African-American Islamic thought. New York: State University of New York Press, 2002

equality and dignity."[52] Often times this embrace of universalism is at the expense of all things culturally black and relevant to the amelioration of the condition of African Americans. African-American universalists transmogrify into Arab-Desi clones, in an effort to be "real Muslims", to the detriment of their own individual agency. Conversely, particularists often stray so far away from the tenants of the faith that Islam becomes unrecognizable in their rituals, customs, and practices.

It is from this ideological dichotomy that Black Islamic organizations such as the Moorish Science Temple and the Nation of Islam arose. These organizations grappled with finding a balance between universalism and particularism in African-American Islamic expression. Timothy Drew (Noble Drew Ali) either by design or default, was probably the first to

---

[52] Curtis, Edward E. Islam in Black America: identity, liberation, and difference in African-American Islamic thought. New York: State University of New York Press, 2002

create an African American Islamic organization that was explicitly particular and the brand of particularism was nationalistic.

Drew Ali was born in 1886 in North Carolina. His birth and childhood are shrouded in mystery but it is believed that he was raised as a black among Cherokee Indians. After becoming a merchant seaman, Drew Ali visited Egypt and took on the title of Noble Drew Ali after passing the test of the Pyramid of Cheops. It is theorized that the title of "noble" and the pyramid test may have been the result of a Masonic initiation. In his book, Black Pilgrimage to Islam, Robert Dannin explores the Masonic connections to the Moorish Science Temple. The organization was divided into two clans, "El" and "Bey". The members greeted each other with "two raised fingers and right hand across the chest, customarily associated with a Masonic greeting."[53] Nevertheless, Drew Ali branded his organization as

---

[53] Dannin, Robert Black Pilgrimage to Islam. Oxford: Oxford University Press, 2002

Bismillah and Bean Pies

Islamic and in 1913 he opened his first temple in Newark called the Canaanite Temple. In 1919 he reorganized and opened a new temple in Chicago. It is here that Drew Ali found success in converting African Americans to his new expression of the Islamic faith. His organization grew with temples established in Detroit, Baltimore, and other cities across the Midwest. Converts were given a strict code of conduct including a prohibition on meat, shaving, intoxicants, and cosmetics.

Drew Ali also produced a "Holy Koran" for his followers. This "Koran" "draws heavily on the legacy of 'classical' black nationalism and teaches a path to spiritual enlightenment based on Christian, Gnostic, Masonic, and Islamic doctrines."[54] His doctrine was a melting of various forms of belief including Masonic, Islamic, and Christian which he used to target, for

---

[54] Miyakawa, Felicia M. Five Percenter Rap: God Hop's Music, Message, and Black Muslim Mission. Indiana: Indiana University Press, 2005

recruitment, newly arriving black southerners into the Midwest.

One of the biggest contributions that the Drew Ali and his Moorish Science Temple gave to black Islamic thought and black nationalism was the idea of blacks in America being Moors. His bridging of these two worlds represented an attempt to separate, if only ideologically, from the United States and to establish a nation. Members were given identity cards that read:

This is your Nationality and Identification Card for the Moorish Science Temple of America, and Birthrights for the Moorish Americans, etc, we honor all the Divine Prophets, Jesus, Mohammed, Buddha, and Confucius. May the blessings of the God our Father Allah, be upon you that carry this card.

It is possible that Ali chose "Moorish" as an identity or nationality after hearing stories of the life of Abd-Al-Rahman Ibrahima.

Bismillah and Bean Pies

The "Moorish Prince", as Ibrahima was known, gained manumission and later fame, when a letter written by Ibrahima fell into the hands of the Moroccan consulate. During his tours of the Eastern United States, Ibrahima's story spread to many African Americans. Another theory is that Drew Ali's father was a Moroccan, whatever the case Drew Ali chose "Moorish" as the nationality of his followers. To the Sunni orthodox Muslim, the inscription on the identity card may be highly problematic but it is an example of black Islamic nationalistic thought and an attempt to balance universalism and particularism. Drew Ali gave to his followers, a nationality. No longer were they simply former slaves void of a history and homeland, they were now Moors and that designation came with a homeland, history, and a religion, Islam. In his work, African American Religion: A Very Short Introduction, Eddie Glaude states "The fact that they called it Islam shows how they participated in a circuit of global exchange—identifying themselves as

Moors or as Asiatics as a means to contest an idea of black people as born in slavery and destined for second-class status and thus connect themselves to a broader current of religious and political meanings." Claude's interpretation of The Moorish Science Temple's teachings and (by default) the Nation of Islam's teaching, gives credence and support to the idea that Islam in black America must be viewed through the prism of nationality and protest of white supremacy and Eurocentric Christianity.

"Although it is difficult to know the extent of Noble Drew Ali's familiarity with the Holy Quran, he understood the rudiments of Muslim practice, which were evident in an emphasis on separation of men and women in the temple, observance of Sabbath on Friday, and daily prayers recited while standing with one's face to the East."[55] Drew Ali's feat becomes truly impressive when it is understood he had little to no contact

---

[55] Dannin, Robert Black Pilgrimage to Islam. Oxford: Oxford University Press, 2002

Bismillah and Bean Pies

with orthodox Islamic practices after leaving Egypt and that Islamic materials such as Quran's or hadith collections were virtually non-existent in the American context nor did he have any teacher of note. He, from sheer will, brought into existence an Islamic expression that lead Bible-based and heavily churched black people into a new religious experience that included a "Koran" and the idea of Islam.

The Moorish science Temple had a set of rituals and practices that were unique to the organization. The men in the organization wore a red fez with a black tassel, grew beards, and were expected to be the main financial support of the women they married. Women were expected to be housewives and to wear modest clothing. They were not allowed to wear makeup and a turban was worn only when they wore long dresses. Every member had to use the surname "El" or "Bey". Unlike traditional Islamic expressions, Moorish Science Temple members prayed three times daily as opposed to five. The members adhered to a strict dietary code only eating vegetables and fish. "Smoking, drinking liquor, straightening the hair, and using cosmetics are forbidden. Sports and games, attendance at motion pictures, and secular dancing are also discouraged."[56]

Nearly twenty years after its inception, high-ranking members of the organization started to take advantage of the members. These men "began to exploit members by selling herbs, magic charms, and literature on the movement."[57] After the death of Drew Ali, inner-fighting caused the movement's

---

[56] Marsh, Clifton E. The Lost-Found Nation of Islam in America. Maryland: ScareCrow Press, 2000

[57] Lee, Martha F. The Nation of Islam: An American Millenarian Movement. New York: Syracuse University Press, 1996

membership to dwindle and then in 1930 a mysterious silk peddler started teaching a new Islamic teaching in the black communities of Detroit that would forever change black Islamic expression. That man was Fard Muhammad.

The Nation of Islam 1930-1975

Imam Wallace D. Muhammad stated "Fard Muhammad studied Noble Drew Ali's approach to introduce the Koran to the black community. Professor Fard introduced the whole text of the Koran, in the very inception of the Nation of Islam. To introduce it he had to put it in the package of Drew Ali." Essentially the Nation of Islam must be viewed as both an ideological and organizational offspring of Marcus Garvey's Universal Negro improvement Association, the Moorish Science Temple, and the traditional black church. This amalgamation created a Christo-Islamic hybrid that was nationalistic, Bible-based, ecclesiastical and used the Quran and Islam as supplements. However, it's formulation the Nation of Islam provided a theology and an expression of Islam that directly addressed the experience of Black Americans in the United States and undoubtedly became the most recognized incarnation of Islam in the country. "The original doctrine of the nation provided a cosmology that fit the experience of many black Americans during the early twentieth century."[58] The Nation of Islam took black protest religion a step further and created a black resignation religion, one that rejected and withdrew from the American social structure and the Christian faith the social structure propagated. The organization expressed its sovereignty by declaring itself to be a "nation within a nation". The Nation of Islam had its own flag, military, national leader, and regions. And just like every nation, the Nation of Islam had its own cuisine including a national pie, the bean pie.

---

[58] Lee, Martha F. The Nation of Islam: An American Millenarian Movement. New York: Syracuse University Press, 1996

Bismillah and Bean Pies

Fard was thought to be of Arab descent although there is some speculation that he may have been Indian and a part of the Ahmadiyya Islamic community. Fanusie theorizes that the Ahmadiyya, in a continued effort to propagate Islam in black America, sent Professor Muhammad Abdullah, under the name W.D. Fard or Fard Muhammad to the United States. Fanusie states that "Professor Muhammad Abdullah was sent as a missionary to the United States by the Ahmadiyya Anjuman Ishaat-i-Islam for the purpose of instructing the Honorable Elijah Muhammed and the Nation of Islam leadership in Islam. Twenty-eight years earlier Abdullah had arrived in the US under the pseudonym W. D. Fard for the purpose of introducing Islam to this same population."[59] Another version of his origin is that he came from Mecca. Sister Clara Muhammad is quoted as saying Fard once said "My name is W.D. Fard, and I come from

---

[59] Fanusie, Fatima "Fard Muhmmad in Historic Context" Lecture Georgetown University March 26, 2014

the Holy City of Mecca. More about myself I will not tell you yet, for the time has not come. I am your brother. You have not yet seen me in my royal robes."[60]

Members of the Nation of Islam believe that Fard was of mixed race, having a black father and a white mother. Despite Nation of Islam's rhetoric against white people and race-mixing, the organization believes that Fard's supposed mixed lineage served to be beneficial because his audience was more receptive to white men propagating religion. "Fard's European features, despite the fact that he presented himself as a mulatto, perhaps made him and his message more palatable to his African-American followers. His light complexion and willingness to take the time to counsel blacks in matters of race and religion probably impressed them more than a similar program sponsored by a conspicuously black man would

---

[60] Beynon, Erdmann D, The Voodoo Cult Among Negro Migrants in Detroit. American Journal of Sociology Illinois: University of Chicago 1938

have."[61] There is also evidence that suggests that Fard was a member of the Moorish Science Temple and that upon the death of Drew Ali, Fard assumed leadership and claimed to be the reincarnation of Drew Ali.[62]

The mystery surrounding Fard is compounded by various police departments and FBI claims about Fard. Law enforcement records attempt to connect Fard with a man named Wallace Ford. According to law enforcement, Fard was born to Hawaiian or British or Polynesian parents in either New Zealand or Portland Oregon. He owned a cafe in California in the 1920's and later spent time in prison for violating a prohibition law and selling narcotics. Upon his release, according to the law enforcement narrative, he moved to Chicago and then to Detroit leaving a

---

[61] Clegg, Claude An Original Man: The Life and Times of Elijah Muhammad. North Carolina: University of North Carolina Press, 1997

[62] Marsh, Clifton E. The Lost-Found Nation of Islam in America. Maryland: ScareCrow Press, 2000

Bismillah and Bean Pies

wife and child in California. The Nation of Islam has historically and categorically denied these claims.

When Fard appeared in black communities in Detroit in the summer of 1930 he did not explicitly propagate the ideas of Islam. Instead, he taught his black customers about the glorious history of their ancestors in their original homeland. "At first the prophet as he came to be known confined his teachings to a recitation of his experiences in foreign lands, admonitions against certain foods, and suggestions for improving his listeners physical health. He was kind friendly unassuming and patient."[63]

Fard did not initially use the Quran as the source material of his teachings. Instead, he relied on the Bible. Fard understood that the black migrant workers arriving in the Midwest were steeped in biblical and church tradition and that any

---

[63] Lincoln, Charles E. The Black Muslims in America. New Jersey: W.M. B. Berdmans Publishing, 1994

Bismillah and Bean Pies

introduction to Islam had to be phased. Fard's pedagogical approach again suggests that his origins may have been Indian, as he propagated Islam in the black community in a similar way to medieval Indian Muslims in Hindu communities. He juxtaposed Islam with traditional black church practice. Fard used the Bible and Christianity as his base and coated his teachings with Islam. Moreover, his teachings contained verbiage that was critical of white society and the racism it propagated. Eventually, the fame of this mysterious silk paddler began to spread throughout Detroit. It is reported that people were converting by the dozens even before the establishment of a permanent temple. "During his ministry from 1930 - 1934 five to eight thousand African Americans joined the Nation of Islam in Detroit and Chicago."[64]

The Great Depression brought over 2,000,000 black people into northern cities seeking a better

---

[64] Berg, Herbert Elijah Muhammad and Islam. New York: New York University Press, 2009

standard of living than in the racially hostile south. Many soon found that northern cities did not provide the expected opportunity of progress due to the same racial prejudices that existed in the South. This created an environment that was fertile and receptive to Fard's message of Islam. "Economic pressure often moves individuals to focus on their religious faith with greater urgency, and in the ghettos, this tendency not surprisingly took on political overtones. Blacks were beginning to emerge from the shadow of slavery, and their religion had, of necessity always served a variety of functions."[65]

Fard's message was potent, nuance, and tailored to the condition of blacks arriving from the South and awakening to the racial realities of the North, he crafted a particularism that would soon become the most recognized expression of Islam in the United States.

---

[65] Lee, Martha F. The Nation of Islam: An American Millenarian Movement. New York: Syracuse University Press, 1996

Bismillah and Bean Pies

The doctrine that Fard formulated was at once a rejection of white supremacy encapsulated in the Christian church and an experiment with psychological reprogramming of his black followers. His pedagogy was aimed at raising the esteem of black people and this "restorative identity was a fundamental tenet of the groups doctrine."[66] His teachings were an amalgamation of previous expressions of both black nationalism and Islam. "Like black separatists, he spoke of African-Americans emigrating back East to avoid extermination and continuing deprivation in America. Similar to Noble Drew Ali, he attempted to transform blacks into Asiatic 'Original People' whose roots were trillions of years old and who had once ruled the earth under the righteous banner of Islam. Additionally, like Mirza Ghulam Ahmad, he presented himself as an intermediary between man and God

---

[66] Lee, Martha F. The Nation of Islam: An American Millenarian Movement. New York: Syracuse University Press, 1996

and later as Allah in person."[67] Fard achieve a great amount of success. "This success led to more formal organizational structures, including a school (the University of Islam), security forces (the Fruit of Islam), domestic training for women (the Girls Training and General Civilization Class), and a second in command (the Supreme Minister of Islam)."[68]

Fard's teachings on the nature of the different races of man were what separated him from any previous black nationalist or Islamist. Fard taught that the nature of the black man(woman) was godly and the nature of the white man (woman)was devilish. Black America had never heard a philosophy the so completely elevated black people and

---

[67] Clegg, Claude An Original Man: The Life and Times of Elijah Muhammad. North Carolina: University of North Carolina Press, 1997

[68] Berg, Herbert Elijah Muhammad and Islam. New York: New York University Press, 2009

simultaneously depreciated whites.[69] At first glance, the teachings appeared to be based on a belief of black supremacy, but when put into context the teachings were an attempt to democratize and bring equity into black theological thought. After centuries of being subject to Christianized white supremacy, Fard's teachings attempted to reconstruct the ideas of race, God, and supremacy in the minds of black people. It was this teaching that attracted thousands of black people to Fard in Detroit including a recently arrived migrant from Georgia named Elijah Poole.

In black Islamic particularism, Elijah Muhammed is the benchmark and standard. The accomplishments during his reign at the helm of the Nation of Islam are unmatched by

---

[69] Bishop Henry McNeal Turner(1934-1915), former chef lord of the African Methodist Episcopal Church and Chancellor of Morris Brown is credited with being the first black clergymen to proclaim "God is a Negro". This was still distinct from Fard's claim that the black man was God.

Bismillah and Bean Pies

any black organization Islamic or not. He lead the organization from 1934-1975. To put his administration into appropriate historical context, in 1934 Dr. Martin Luther King was five years old and Malcolm X was nine and when Elijah Muhammed died in 1975 Dr. King had been deceased for seven years and Malcolm X a full decade.

Elijah Muhammed was born Elijah Pool in Sandersville Georgia in 1897. He was the seventh son of a sharecropper named William Poole and his wife Marie. William is said to have been a mulatto and "his caramel-colored complexion placed him among the "privileged" freedmen in the South, meaning he received a Bible-based education, but he was nonetheless only marginally literate."[70] William was also a

---

[70] Evanzz, Karl The Messenger: the rise and fall of Elijah Muhmmad. New York: Random House, 1999

Bismillah and Bean Pies

minister at Zion Hope Baptist Church.[71]

William and Marie(Mariah) had a total of twelve children in economically depressed rural Georgia. The family briefly moved to Arkansas with the hopes of opportunity but soon returned to Cordele Georgia where Elijah attended the Holdey-Cobb Institute, a Methodist school, headed by Bishop Turner.[72] "Shortly after he started school at the age of six, Elijah's demeanor changed. Once a very active child, he suddenly became quiet and introverted, often parking himself in a corner of the living room with the Holy Bible the minute he finished his homework and after-school chores."[73]

---

[71] According to Claude A. Clegg in "The Life and Times of Elijah Muhammad William Poole pastored Spring Baptist Church and Union Baptist Church in Cordele, GA

[72] see footnote 69

[73] Evanzz, Karl The Messenger: the rise and fall of Elijah Muhmmad. New York: Random House, 1999

Bismillah and Bean Pies

As a child, Elijah was troubled by many experiences in the church. The narratives of hell fire and slave hymns had a profound impact on the young Elijah. He suffered nightmares because of these experiences. Elijah Muhammad is quoted as saying his father's sermons were "so frightening until I, myself, being his son, would tremble...I would think and wonder, 'will I live to get to heaven before this comes?'".[74] Elijah developed an impassioned curiosity for the Christian doctrine and the understanding of God, faith, and predestination.

The world that shaped Elijah's childhood was filled with trauma. Lynchings, KKK attacks, and the literal imprisonment of an African man in a monkey cage at the Bronx Zoo colored Elijah's perception of the world. He lived in time of growing racial hostilities marked with lynch mobs and a daily fear of white aggression. These things coupled

---

[74] Clegg, Claude An Original Man: The Life and Times of Elijah Muhammad. North Carolina: University of North Carolina Press, 1997

with debt slavery and peonage resonated with Elijah. At age ten, Elijah witnessed the lynching of an eighteen-year-old that he had known. "The murder and the subdued reaction of the African American community repulsed him, and his tears flowed unencumbered. He cried for the dead youth and the rest of the blacks of Cordele, who had, in his view allowed the killing to take place."[75]

During the years 1914-1924, a series of factors forced thousands of blacks to leave the rural south. An uptick in lynchings, a boll weevil infestation, and the outbreak of World War I, which created industrial jobs in the North, forced blacks into the Great Migration. "In April 1923, Elijah, Clara(wife) and their children migrated...to Detroit, Michigan."[76]

---

[75] Clegg, Claude An Original Man: The Life and Times of Elijah Muhammad. North Carolina: University of North Carolina Press, 1997

[76] Clegg, Claude An Original Man: The Life and Times of Elijah Muhammad. North Carolina: University of North Carolina Press, 1997

Bismillah and Bean Pies

When the family arrived in Detroit, Elijah stayed with his parents, who also migrated to Detroit, before he found work at the American Nut Company. The industrial North proved to be just as challenging as the rural South. Elijah soon realized that his salary, although double what he made in the south, could only afford the same standard of living in Detroit. The family moved into a small apartment with a very cramped living space.

Elijah also discovered that the KKK had a very large and active membership in the North and often terrorized black communities there as they did in Georgia. This prompted blacks to join groups such as Marcus Garvey's Universal Negro Improvement Association. Elijah, seeing the UNIA as a formidable response to the KKK, joined the organization. But by the time Elijah joined the UNIA, Garvey was arrested and the organization was in peril.

Bismillah and Bean Pies

Seeking another refuge, Elijah joined the all black Ancient Egyptian Order of the Nobles of the Mystic Shrine of the North and South America. This black Freemasonry organization was a large bureaucracy and soon Elijah realized he would never be more than low-level member and he soon left the organization. There is speculation by Robert Dannin that Drew Ali and Elijah Muhammad's membership in Freemasonry organizations helped to shaped the structure of their respective groups.

The combination of employment struggles, the inability to provide enough for his family, and the disappointment with black organizations contributed to Elijah developing a serious addiction to alcohol. Often times he would spend Friday nights drinking to the point of passing out. He was arrested for public intoxication and swore off alcohol only to start drinking again several weeks later. The alcoholism soon took a toll on his marriage and Clara insisted Elijah stop drinking.

Bismillah and Bean Pies

During this time, Elijah's interest in the ministry and religion was fed by discussions with his father and brother Billie. One day his father mentioned a conversation he had with a man named Abdul Muhammad about the faith of Islam as taught by Fard Muhammad. This sparked Elijah's interest and soon he met several times with Abdul to learn more about Fard's message. Elijah did not immediately attend any of Fard's gatherings as he had reservations about the religion of Islam and perceived it negatively because of his Christian sensibilities.

In 1931, Elijah attended his first meeting to hear Fard's message. "According to Elijah, thousands of people had appeared for this meeting, and he, like the others could only hear parts of the teacher's speech. Nevertheless, he was still able to hear enough of the message to gain a sense of Fard's Islam and what it meant to him and the black community in Detroit."[77] Elijah was convinced that Fard's message was the truth and soon became a faithful follower of Fard, who was now claiming to be Jesus and the Mahdi prophesied to come in Islamic tradition.

Elijah's childhood experiences witnessing the horrific acts of lynchings made Fard's teaching of "white devils" palatable and reasonable. Furthermore, Fard's teachings of black superiority during the depression era came as a psychological relief from the daily struggle Elijah and many blacks endured.

Elijah became Fard's most faithful student and was soon named as the Supreme Minister which equated to being second in command. Soon Fard started to fade from the public eye and in 1934 Elijah took the helm of leadership.

---

[77] Clegg, Claude An Original Man: The Life and Times of Elijah Muhammad. North Carolina: University of North Carolina Press, 1997

Elijah Poole became Elijah Karriem then Elijah Muhammad and the chief propagator of "Fardian Islam". The teachings were black nationalism, black Christianity and Islam converged. This completely new expression of Islam was unique to black Americans and was virtually unknown to the rest of the Islamic world. "Elijah Muhammad claimed that almost all of his teachings came directly from Fard Muhammad, even decades later. The teachings of Fard Muhammad as summarized by Elijah Muhammad included knowledge of 'ourselves, of Himself(God) and the devil, the measurement of the Earth, other planets and the civilization of some of the planets other than Earth...the history of the moon, the history of the two nations the dominate the earth, black and white.'"[78] Furthermore, the idea of a mad scientist named Yakub grafting the white race on an Island in the Aegean Sea and turning the "black nation" against itself was a foreign concept to Sunni orthodox Islam, yet

---

[78] Berg, Herbert Elijah Muhammad and Islam. New York: New York University Press, 2009

this form of Islamic particularism resonated with the black populations of the Midwest and eventually throughout black America. On the other hand, some Fardian Islamic teachings are in line with orthodoxy, including prayer practices, a prohibition against pork, gambling, and alcohol, Mecca being a holy city and the Quran being a holy book.

"The mention of Mecca, Moses, Jesus, and Muhammad may seem to be mere superficial references to traditional Islam. Yet it is important that Islam, if not its traditional Arabian mythology, still plays a central role in this race myth. It is the natural religion of the 'black man', it is the religion of the prophets, and it is as old as Allah and the universe. More importantly, it stands in opposition to Christianity, which 'is one of the most perfect black-slave-making religions on our planet."[79]

---

[79] Berg, Herbert Elijah Muhammad and Islam. New York: New York University Press, 2009

Bismillah and Bean Pies

Under Elijah Muhammad, the Nation of Islam would write a chapter in the American narrative that would have a long-lasting impact on the country and the Islamic world. The organization is arguably that most successful black nationalist organization in history. Muhammad's leadership oversaw the building of a nationwide infrastructure that included schools, an international import business, bakeries, office buildings, print shops and a black national newspaper. "Wherever Muslims lived, they established small business associated with the local temple, including barbershops, bakeries, clothing stores and restaurants. Many non-Muslims patronized these establishments. Still, more businesses were owned personally by Elijah Muhammad, who presided over a multimillion-dollar business empire which consisted of a printing press, farms, restaurants, a meat packing plant, homes, apartments, trucks, a clothing factory and a small bank."[80] Yet, his most impressive product was his cadre of students which include some of the most well-known black men in the world. Malcolm X, Louis Farrakhan, W.D. Muhammad and, the most famous of all, Muhammad Ali are all students of the man they called the honorable Elijah Muhammad.

During the reign of Elijah Muhammad many immigrant Muslims condemned the Nation of Islam and labeled the organization as heretics. Groups such as the Islamic Center of Washington(D.C.) denied the Islamic legitimacy of the group. Other African American Muslims leaders, such as Talib Ahmad Dawud, agreed with the Elijah Muhammad's views on separatism but rejected the notion of Fard as Allah and the "denial of a future, bodily resurrection, and his followers

---

[80] Curtis, Edward E. Black Muslim religion in the Nation of Islam, 1960-1975. North Carolina: University of North Carolina Press, 2006

failure to adhere to proper Muslim prayer rituals."[81]

While the Nation of Islam's expression of Islam can be critiqued, there is little room for denial of the organization's impact on Islam in the American context. "They practiced their religion not only by reciting prayers and their creeds but also by paying attention to what they ate, how they dressed, and what music they listened to. For NOI practitioners, Islam was not only a theology but also a system of ritualized practices that brought them what they described as dignity, hope, civilization, self-determination, pride, peace, security, and salvation."[82] The Nation of Islam's brand of Islamic particularism addressed the concerns, conditions,

---

[81] Curtis, Edward E. Black Muslim religion in the Nation of Islam, 1960-1975. North Carolina: University of North Carolina Press, 2006

[82] Curtis, Edward E. Black Muslim religion in the Nation of Islam, 1960-1975. North Carolina: University of North Carolina Press, 2006

and unique experience of black Americans.

After the death of Elijah Muhammad in 1975, his son Warith Deen Muhammad, known as Imam Warith Deen, took over the leadership of the Nation of Islam. He drastically changed the make-up of the organization. Warith Deen, who was learned in the tenants of orthodoxy, rebranded his father's organization and named it "The World Community of al-Islam in the West." Warith Deen denounced his father's teachings on race and religion and embraced the views of Sunni Islam. He disbanded the Fruit of Islam, implemented traditional Islamic prayer rituals, renamed the temples, and adapted the dress code. Most shockingly he rejected the belief of Fard Muhammad as Allah or Elijah Muhammad as the messenger of Allah. These acts effectively moved the organization into mainstream Islamic teachings but with a particular black consciousness.

Nevertheless, these changes proved to be too much for some of the followers of Elijah Muhammad and in 1978, a group led by Louis Farrakhan separated from the World Community of al-Islam and reorganized under the banner of the Nation of Islam. Farrakhan reestablished the Fruit of Islam and the teachings of Elijah Muhammad but with a new Islamic consciousness.

For forty years, black Islamic expression has existed somewhere in the center of this dichotomy attempting to find a balance between the universal and the particular, separatism and inclusion, mainstream and counterculture with both communities embracing, in some fashion, nationalism, orthodoxy, and the bean pie.

Citations

1. Glaude Jr., Eddie S. African American Religion: A Very Short Introduction. Oxford: Oxford University Press, 2014.

2. Curtis, EE Muslims In America: A Short History. Oxford: Oxford University Press, 2009

3. Curtis, EE Muslims In America: A Short History. Oxford: Oxford University Press, 2009

4. Hill, Margari The Spread of Islam in West Africa: Containment, Mixing, and Reform from the Eighth to the Twentieth Century. Stanford: Stanford University, 2009

5. Diop, Cheik A. Precolonial Black Africa. Illinois: Chicago Review Press, 1987

6. Diouf, Sylviane A. Servants of Allah: African Muslims Enslaved in the Americas. New York: New York UP, 1998

7. Hill, Margari The Spread of Islam in West Africa: Containment, Mixing, and Reform from the Eighth to the Twentieth Century. Stanford: Stanford University, 2009

8. Hill, Margari The Spread of Islam in West Africa: Containment, Mixing, and Reform from the Eighth to the Twentieth Century. Stanford: Stanford University, 2009

9. Tschanz, David W. Lion of Mali: The Hajj of Mansa Musa. http://www.academia.edu/1593503/Lion_Of_Mali_The_Hajj_of_Mansa_Musa 2012

10. Tschanz, David W. Lion of Mali: The Hajj of Mansa Musa. http://www.academia.edu/1593503/Lion_Of_Mali_The_Hajj_of_Mansa_Musa 2012

11. Moreau, Rene L. Africains Musulmans. Paris: Presence Africaine, 1982

12. Diouf, Sylviane A. Servants of Allah: African Muslims Enslaved in the Americas. New York: New York UP, 1998

13. Diouf, Sylviane A. Servants of Allah: African Muslims Enslaved in the Americas. New York: New York UP, 1998

14. Phrase coined by Dr. Michael Eric Dyson. It implies conducting unprovoked aggressive action based on the idea that one might be attacked in the future.

15. Gallaudet, T. H. A statement with regard to the Moorish prince Abduhl Rahhahman. New York: appointed to solicit Subscriptions in New York to aid redeeming the Family of the Prince from Slavery, 1828.

16. "Muslims in Early Georgia: Introduction." Http://libguides.ccga.edu/muslims. College of Coastal Georgia Libraries, 20 June 2016.

17. Alkhateeb, Firas. "The First Muslim-American Scholar: Bilali Muhammad." Lost Islamic History. Web. <lostislamichistory.com> 24 Feb 2014.

18. Alkhateeb, Firas. "The First Muslim-American Scholar: Bilali Muhammad." Lost Islamic History. Web. <lostislamichistory.com> 24 Feb 2014.

19. King, Colbert. "Yarrow Mamout, the slave who became a Georgetown financier." The Washington Post. Web. <washingtonpost.com/opinions/yarrow-mamout>

20. Johnston, John H. From Slave Ship to Harvard: Yarrow Mamout and the History of an African American Family. New York: Fordham University Press, 2010

21. Curtis, Edward E. Islam in Black America: identity, liberation, and difference in African-American Islamic thought. New York: State University of New York Press, 2002

22. Pawlikova-Vilhanova, Viera Christianity, Islam and the African world: Edward Wilmot Blyden(1832-1912) and contemporary missionary thought. Institute of Oriental and African Studies, Slovak Academy of Sciences, 2002 pg 117-128

23. Pawlikova-Vilhanova, Viera Christianity, Islam and the African world: Edward Wilmot Blyden(1832-1912) and contemporary missionary thought. Institute of Oriental and African Studies, Slovak Academy of Sciences, 2002 pg 117-128

24. Curtis, Edward E. Islam in Black America: identity, liberation, and difference in African-American Islamic thought. New York: State University of New York Press, 2002

25. Pawlikova-Vilhanova, Viera Christianity, Islam and the African world: Edward Wilmot Blyden(1832-1912) and contemporary missionary thought. Institute of Oriental and African

Studies, Slovak Academy of Sciences, 2002 pg 117-128

26.Curtis, Edward E. Islam in Black America: identity, liberation, and difference in African-American Islamic thought. New York: State University of New York Press, 2002

27. Haddad, Yvonne Y. Esposito, John L. Muslims on the Americanization Path?. New York: Oxford University Press

28. Haddad, Yvonne Y. Smith, Jane I. Muslim Minorities in the West. Oxford: Altamira Press, 2002

29. Turner, Richard Brent Islam in the African American Experience . Indiana: Indiana University Press 1997, 2003

30. Evanzz, Karl The Messenger: the rise and fall of Elijah Muhmmad. New York: Random House, 1999

31.Hill, Robert A and Garvey, Marcus The Marcus Garvey and Universal Negro Improvement Association

Papers. California: University of
California Press, 1991

32. Van Deburg, William L. Modern
Black Nationalism: From Marcus
Garvey to Louis Farrakhan. New
York: New York University Press,
1997

33. Turner, Richard Brent Islam in
the African American Experience .
Indiana: Indiana University Press
1997, 2003

34. Hill, Robert A and Garvey, Marcus
The Marcus Garvey and Universal
Negro Improvement Association
Papers. California: University of
California Press, 1991

35. Van Deburg, William L. Modern
Black Nationalism: From Marcus
Garvey to Louis Farrakhan. New
York: New York University Press,
1997

36. Turner, Richard Brent Islam in
the African American Experience.
Indiana: Indiana University Press
1997, 2003

37. Turner, Richard Brent Islam in the African American Experience. Indiana: Indiana University Press 1997, 2003

38. Haddad, Yvonne Y. Smith, Jane I. Muslim Minorities in the West. Oxford: Altamira Press, 2002

39. Berg, Herbert Elijah Muhammad and Islam. New York: New York University Press, 2009

40. Berg, Herbert Elijah Muhammad and Islam. New York: New York University Press, 2009

41. Gibson, Dawn-Marie A History of the Nation of Islam: Race, Islam, and the Quest for Freedom. California: ABC-CLIO, 2012

42. McCloud, Aminah Beverly African American Islam. New York: Routledge, 1995

43. Fanusie, Fatima "Fard Muhmmad in Historic Context" Lecture

Georgetown University March 26, 2014

44. Curtis, Edwards E. Islamism and its African American Muslim Critics: Black Muslims in the Era of the Arab Cold War. American Quarterly Journal 2007

45. Gibson, Dawn-Marie A History of the Nation of Islam: Race, Islam, and the Quest for Freedom. California: ABC-CLIO, 2012

46. McCloud, Aminah Beverly African American Islam. New York: Routledge, 1995

47. McCloud, Aminah Beverly African American Islam. New York: Routledge, 1995

48. McCloud, Aminah Beverly African American Islam. New York: Routledge, 1995

49. Curtis, Edwards E. Islamism and its African American Muslim Critics: Black Muslims in the Era of the Arab

Cold War. American Quarterly Journal 2007

50. Curtis, Edwards E. Islamism and its African American Muslim Critics: Black Muslims in the Era of the Arab Cold War. American Quarterly Journal 2007

51. Curtis, Edward E. Islam in Black America: identity, liberation, and difference in African-American Islamic thought. New York: State University of New York Press, 2002

52. Curtis, Edward E. Islam in Black America: identity, liberation, and difference in African-American Islamic thought. New York: State University of New York Press, 2002

53. Dannin, Robert Black Pilgrimage to Islam. Oxford: Oxford University Press, 2002

54. Miyakawa, Felicia M. Five Percenter Rap: God Hop's Music, Message, and Black Muslim Mission. Indiana: Indiana University Press, 2005

55. Dannin, Robert Black Pilgrimage to Islam. Oxford: Oxford University Press, 2002

56. Marsh, Clifton E. The Lost-Found Nation of Islam in America. Maryland: ScareCrow Press, 2000

57. Lee, Martha F. The Nation of Islam: An American Millenarian Movement. New York: Syracuse University Press, 1996

58. Lee, Martha F. The Nation of Islam: An American Millenarian Movement. New York: Syracuse University Press, 1996

59. Fanusie, Fatima "Fard Muhmmad in Historic Context" Lecture Georgetown University March 26, 2014

60. Beynon, Erdmann D, The Voodoo Cult Among Negro Migrants in Detroit. American Journal of Sociology Illinois: University of Chicago 1938

61. Clegg, Claude An Original Man: The Life and Times of Elijah Muhammad. North Carolina: University of North Carolina Press, 1997

62. Marsh, Clifton E. The Lost-Found Nation of Islam in America. Maryland: ScareCrow Press, 2000

63. Lincoln, Charles E. The Black Muslims in America. New Jersey: W.M. B. Berdmans Publishing, 1994

64. Berg, Herbert Elijah Muhammad and Islam. New York: New York University Press, 2009

65. Lee, Martha F. The Nation of Islam: An American Millenarian Movement. New York: Syracuse University Press, 1996

66. Lee, Martha F. The Nation of Islam: An American Millenarian Movement. New York: Syracuse University Press, 1996

67. Clegg, Claude An Original Man: The Life and Times of Elijah

Muhammad. North Carolina: University of North Carolina Press, 1997

68. Berg, Herbert Elijah Muhammad and Islam. New York: New York University Press, 2009

69. Bishop Henry McNeal Turner(1934-1915), former chef lord of the African Methodist Episcopal Church and Chancellor of Morris Brown is credited with being the first black clergymen to proclaim "God is a Negro". This was still distinct from Fard's claim that the black man was God.

70. Evanzz, Karl The Messenger: the rise and fall of Elijah Muhmmad. New York: Random House, 1999

71. According to Claude A. Clegg in "The Life and Times of Elijah Muhammad William Poole pastored Spring Baptist Church and Union Baptist Church in Cordele, GA

72. see footnote 69

73. Evanzz, Karl The Messenger: the rise and fall of Elijah Muhmmad. New York: Random House, 1999

74. Clegg, Claude An Original Man: The Life and Times of Elijah Muhammad. North Carolina: University of North Carolina Press, 1997

75. Clegg, Claude An Original Man: The Life and Times of Elijah Muhammad. North Carolina: University of North Carolina Press, 1997

76. Clegg, Claude An Original Man: The Life and Times of Elijah Muhammad. North Carolina: University of North Carolina Press, 1997

77. Clegg, Claude An Original Man: The Life and Times of Elijah Muhammad. North Carolina: University of North Carolina Press, 1997

78. Berg, Herbert Elijah Muhammad and Islam. New York: New York University Press, 2009

79. Berg, Herbert Elijah Muhammad and Islam. New York: New York University Press, 2009

80. Curtis, Edward E. Black Muslim religion in the Nation of Islam, 1960-1975. North Carolina: University of North Carolina Press, 2006

81. Curtis, Edward E. Black Muslim religion in the Nation of Islam, 1960-1975. North Carolina: University of North Carolina Press, 2006

82. Curtis, Edward E. Black Muslim religion in the Nation of Islam, 1960-1975. North Carolina: University of North Carolina Press, 2006

Made in the USA
Middletown, DE
30 April 2025